SKI TALES

The History of China Peak and Sierra Summit

SKI TALES

The History of China Peak and Sierra Summit

JAMES A. BENELLI

Fresno, CA

Ski Tales: The History of China Peak and Sierra Summit

All photos are by the author, unless otherwise noted.

Published by Craven Street Books,
an imprint of Linden Publishing.
2006 S. Mary, Fresno, California, 93721
559-233-6633 / 800-345-4447
CravenStreetBooks.com

Craven Street Books is a trademark of Linden Publishing, Inc.

Craven Street Books project cadre: Jaguar Bennett, Kent Sorsky.
Typeset by Vikatan Publishing Solutions (P) Ltd., Chennai, India
Printed in the USA on acid-free paper.

ISBN: 978-1-884995-66-8
35798642

Contents

Dedicated to Evan, Chris, Audrey, Jessica, and Madeline.

CHAPTER 1

An Overview

Trying to explain a ski area to a person who is not a skier, and not a mountain person, would be like describing an elephant to a person who has never seen one—or attempting to paint a word picture of Las Vegas to my ninety-year-old aunt who has never left her home state of Kansas.

Speaking to skiers, however, is a horse of another color. We relish the challenge of the steepest slopes, the pristine whiteness of a snow-covered trail, clear air, and the camaraderie with souls of like persuasion. We are the unique individuals who beg the snow-gods to send us more of the white stuff. We are the mountain people who live in our own dream world, with our skis always at the ready, waxed, and standing in the corner. We are the die-hards that, when the weatherman warns of a winter storm, we only hear, "Gentlemen, start your engines."

When we were younger, we were the heartier and toughest of the ski breed. We have even been suspected of sleeping in our cars in the parking lot to be first on the slopes. Some of us are fortunate enough to live out our dreams in mountain homes, ready to ski at the drop of a hat. Others of us must live the more mundane life of the unfortunate eight-to-fiver. Many are stuck in offices in the valley and unable to even see mountains. Skiing is the precious escape from the structured business life to the charming world of the weekend skier.

I am a skier! It's pure and simple. When I mention the mountain people who love the winter, the cold, the snow, and the blue skies, I am speaking to skiers, boarders, picnickers, and snowman builders. We all share the common bond of the mountain. We are kindred spirits that the flat-landers find curious and will never understand. We cultivate friends who ski like us: the powder-hounds who are at the top of the class, followed by the racers, the down-hillers, the cross-country people, down to the corduroy freaks that savor the smooth grooming that turns mediocrity into expertness.

Sierra Summit is the Holy Grail to us. It revives our spirits, our very being—almost like a short trip to the Vatican to cleanse our souls of the very sins of working. We are the locals who are unimpressed with the mega-resorts owned by giant ski corporations. We need skiing close to home, where our hard-earned dollars have more mileage than the Squaw Valleys and Mammoths of the world. We don't need luxurious surroundings—we are as happy as clams when we brown-bag it at picnic tables. Fine wine is for sissies. We like Budweiser in cans. Four-wheel-drive pickups fill our parking lots. Porsches and Caddies are tolerated, but they must park with the riff-raff, and should not expect special treatment.

Sierra Summit, which started life as China Peak, is our kind of place. I am honored to be asked to write the story of how and why a resort is here at all. I don't intend for my book to look like a stockholder's report, to paint a colorful picture of the resort's past, or to lay out optimistic projections for future profits. It will not outline the business of managing a ski resort, for I do not profess to have these skills. However, this will be the true history of Sierra Summit, its successes and shortcomings, and the interesting folks who have nurtured it into what it is today. This is more of a commentary on people than real estate. The skiing public, especially the ski professionals whom I have met and worked with during my years of skiing, consists of more than a few interesting characters.

I have been very fortunate to have been a skier at China Peak-Sierra Summit every season since 1960—as of this writing, forty-eight years. I have been a ski-bum, a customer, a ski instructor, a National Ski Patrolman, a Pro Patrolman, and a bartender, all in an undying effort to ski more days than the previous year while spending less money. Each ski day, to

"I have seen with impartial eyes, and I am sure I have written at least honestly, whether wisely or not."
—Mark Twain, 1869

The author, better known to friends as Jim, in his official ski school uniform. This was the first uniform with the new Sierra Summit logo, issued in 1982..

me, is an opportunity that cannot be bypassed. It may never come again. The fisherman knows that this is the day the big one will bite; the golfer knows he might hit a hole-in-one. As a skier, I know each day will be the best day of my ski life; the day I make only perfect turns, all flawlessly linked, and timed like exquisite music.

I have known every manager of this hill from Knute Flint, the builder, to Brian Bressel, the present manager. I have marveled at the ski artistry of such greats as Stan Beach, who departed this world much too soon due to cancer. I have taught skiing in the fast-paced school under the directorship of Phil Kerridge, who, still to this day, I consider the best technical skier I have ever skied with. I have had the privilege of working in the National Ski Patrol with Billy McCullum and Ralph Lockwood, two of the many patrollers who have made the Sierra Summit Ski Patrol what it is today, the best in the west. I watched in awe as tiny Mary Wren, in her sixties, and her daughter, Rindy, both expert patrollers, loaded an injured 200-pound man in a sled and took him down the Face. Straight down the Face! For those who may not be in the know, the Face is the steepest run on the mountain. It is seldom groomed, and it humbles even the strongest skier. It is a black diamond, meant for experts only. Sierra Summit patrollers are the best.

In the early days of China Peak, many of the instructors were European, and they expected to be looked up to, and treated, like ski gods. They were prima-donnas in every sense of the word. They walked with their noses in the air, and generally looked with dismay at skiers of lesser ability. I was one of the latter. I liked teaching skiing, and made no bones about not being the hottest of the hot. Phil Kerridge ran China Peak Ski School like the schools in Europe where he had been trained. He demanded the utmost respect from his underlings, and expected them to perform like he did.

My best friend in the ski school was Bob Soares, who unfortunately also lost a battle with cancer too early in life. (Bob was buried in his ski clothes, at his request.) He was fed up with the business life—he had been an executive with UPS. About the same time that I took early retirement from my airline, he left his company. He and I had both been teaching skiing part-time, and we decided to teach full-time. Bob was a great teacher; he loved people, worked hard, and enjoyed life to the fullest. He was tall, tanned and handsome, with coal-black hair that was graying at the temples. He was the ultimate ski-instructor. He was not, however, the greatest skier. Phil Kerridge really thought that if his instructors tried

The ski school director doing his job, showing a group of instructors how it's done. Notice that they are paying rapt attention, envious and willing to learn by watching the master, trying to catch the intricate weight shifts and subtle moves, here performed with perfection. *Photo courtesy Phil Kerridge collection.*

just a bit harder, they could ski perfectly, just like he did. This was a good thought, but things rarely worked out that way.

Phil took about ten instructors out early one morning for our regular dose of humiliation. We warmed up with some fast skiing, and ended up on Dynamite, a medium-steep hill with a few moguls. We all lined up at the top where Phil gave his usual pep-talk. He was going to ski down to Academy, where he would stop and watch each instructor ski down individually, and judge their performance. Phil skied down perfectly, stopped, and turned facing the hill, basking in his glory. He waved a ski pole, the signal for the first instructor to go. That guy turned in a perfect run; not a single mistake. Each instructor skied down better than the one before. All showed perfect balance and timing. Bob and I kept moving to the back of the line. Finally, there was no one left but Bob and me. All the others were at the bottom watching. Bob said, "You go." I said, "No, you go." Phil was waving his ski pole impatiently. Finally, I went. To my total surprise, my skiing was flawless and I performed perfectly. Bob was the only one left at the top; he could not postpone the pain any longer. He took a deep breath and shoved off. His first turn was good, but then he seemed to move back on his skis. At each turn he took he tried to catch up, and that just made it worse. Halfway down the hill, he lost it completely. First, he went up on one ski, and then the other. Sheer panic painted his face. Painfully, as if in slow motion, he went down and started tumbling. Both skis released and took off on their own.

Phil, the other instructors, and I stood at the bottom of the hill. We were watching in horror at the catastrophe unfolding on the hill. Bob came sliding down, yelling, "Look out!" Our little group scattered out of the way as fast as we could to escape this certain collision. All, that is, except Phil. Bob hit him dead on. He hit him so hard he knocked Phil clean out of his skis, and they slid together for what seemed to be forever. They finally stopped and untangled themselves. It was a miracle that nobody was injured. Phil was furious, but before he had a chance to say a word, Bob wiped the snow off his face, and drawled, "god dammit, Phil, if you hadn't been in my way, I could have recovered."

THE FIRST DAYS

Where did Sierra Summit come from? How did it come in to being? Who started all this business of a ski resort here, anyway? Does it really matter? Should today's snow-boarders even care about a bit of California History that put affordable skiing in their own backyard?

You bet they should! Especially when they realize that the people who built this place were fascinating, interesting people. They would have to be, or they wouldn't have been in the ski business in the first place. There were other ski resorts in the state—were there enough skiers here in the 1950s to support another area? Was the sport really here to stay, or would it be a passing fancy that would come and go? After all, we could have enjoyed the mountains and the snow without ski trails and chairlifts. People have been climbing around them for a hundred years. Before we explore the fascinating history of China Peak and Sierra Summit, let's take a brief look at some of the other ski resorts in the central Sierra Nevada Mountains.

MAMMOTH MOUNTAIN

Dave McCoy had a permit to operate a portable rope tow on the eastern slope of the Sierra since 1941, and he built his first permanent rope tow on the north side of the mountain in 1945. In 1954, McCoy received a twenty-five-year use permit under the condition that he begin to develop the mountain. By the mid-50s, Mammoth was attracting more skiers than any other California operation. Dave's ski schools and race training were legendary. Skiers by the hundreds were willingly driving the 350 miles from Los Angeles to ski

China Peak's 1973–1974 brochure featured three chair lifts, two T-bars and a rope tow. A ticket for all lifts was $7.50.

Mammoth on weekends. The lift lines and traffic jams were horrific, even by Los Angeles standards.

BADGER PASS

Yosemite Park & Curry Company, the concessionaire that operated within Yosemite National Park, had established the Yosemite Winter Club in 1928 "to encourage the development of all winter sports." They created a small ski hill and a ski jump near the Tenaya Creek Bridge, and organized a ski school under the direction of Jules Frisch. The opening of the Wawona Tunnel in 1934, and the Glacier Point Road to Badger Pass in 1935, made the ski area possible. By 1935, Badger Pass was welcoming 30,000 skiers annually. Some of the instructors in the early days of Badger Pass went on to pioneer skiing in the west's best-known ski resorts. Sigi Engl went to Sun Valley, Hannes Schroll to Sugar Bowl, and Luggi Foeger to Donner Summit. Nic Fiore, the popular French-Canadian, arrived in Yosemite in 1948 as a ski instructor, and soon worked his way up to ski school director. Nic is legendary, his name synonymous with Badger Pass, and he built it to what it is today. Badger Pass is a small area, and being located in Yosemite National Park, it has no space to expand. It had always been popular with the social elite, and was a weekend getaway for San Franciscans, as well as a destination resort for Easterners.

Our nearby Sierra Nevada range has offered winter escapes for adventurous outdoor people for many years. Snowshoeing and winter hiking were popular sports for the hearty, but skiers had to hike up steep slopes to get any downhill coasting. Skiing was becoming popular in the east, and the new resorts in the west were gaining many followers. There were enough ski enthusiasts in the Fresno area to form the Fresno Ski Club in 1934. A new ski area in the central Sierra near Fresno was mentioned in the *Fresno Bee* as early as February, 1946, in an article by Omer Crane. Planning was underway, but winter access was a major factor, as roads in the area were not always passable, due to heavy drifting snowstorms.

Skiing was becoming more and more popular in California, and the need was increasing for more access to the Sierra Nevada Mountains. Fresno City and the County Chamber of Commerce executive secretary M.P. Loshe had long pushed for a resort near Huntington Lake. He was not a skier, but he was an avid snowshoer and an outdoorsman. The new highway between Shaver Lake and Huntington Lake was completed in the summer of 1956. The old hairpin curves on the road by way of Big Creek had been eliminated. The new road bypassed Big Creek altogether, and went from Shaver Lake to Huntington. The road was now wide enough that the new rotary snowplows could now keep it relatively snow free through the winter. At least the roads would be passable.

The Forest Service was also favorable to the idea of another ski area. The mountains near Huntington Lake had been scouted for a ski area in 1954. Tom Sovulewski, a native of Yosemite and twice state Alpine champion in the mid-1930s, led rangers of the Sierra National Forest as they searched the Fresno County back country for an ideal ski site.

"This is the place," declared scout Sovulewski, and Sierra National Forest supervisor Leon Thomas agreed. They were standing on an area sloping toward Big Creek at the southwest corner of Huntington Lake, on a ridge which was crowned by a volcanic plug and listed on the Forest Service maps as "Chinese Peak." The location for the new ski area had been decided on. It was now time to turn this dream into a reality.

This familiar machine is a welcome sight after a storm, keeping highway 168 open for skiers and travelers to Sierra Summit and Huntington Lake.

CHAPTER 2

China Peak: The Beginning

"**D**ream Will Come True in China Peak Resort," shouted the headlines in *The Fresno Bee* sports page, on Sunday, August 19, 1956. "$1,000,000 Winter Playground Will Be Built By 35 Year Old Financial Genius. Knute Flint had signed the contract with Leon Thomas of the Sierra National Forest for the conditional use permit. It's now official."

The very mention of interesting characters must start with this first dreamer, schemer, and entrepreneur. Was he just a lucky guy who happened to be in the right place at the right time, or did he possess the far-sightedness necessary to transform a dream into a world-class resort? Actually, he did have the foresight to build it, but keeping it going through thick and thin years would prove even more difficult than the Herculean task of moving mountains to build ski trails.

Knute Flint was an ex-Army helicopter pilot. He was brash, young, and possessed boundless energy. He often read books while driving. He was, in fact, stopped by the California Highway Patrol for doing just that. He explained to the officer that this would not be safe for most people, but that he was perfectly capable of doing two things at once. The officer let him go with just a warning.

Flint had made a fortune in the rough and tumble business of operating helicopters, primarily in the infancy stage of forest fire protection. He started by buying two used Bell 47 helicopters and modified them for forest fire work. He then sold his services on contract to the U.S. Forest Service. Flint was smart, creative, and shrewd. He knew how to get things done, and had patents on several inventions intended to make helicopters carry heavier loads. Although none of his ideas ever made it to market, they were very interesting. One consisted of a Helium-filled balloon, towed by a helicopter; the combination could lift a heavier load than the totals either could lift individually.

Flint moved his family to Paris, and he ran his international helicopter operation from there. His two children were fluent in French and English. The ski industry intrigued Flint, and he and his family had skied at all the top resorts in Europe. He was originally from the Los Angeles area, and was familiar with U.S. Forest Service contracts. He enjoyed a good reputation for fair dealing, which was rather rare in the early days of helicopter service. When he got wind of the possible agreement for another ski area, he jumped at the chance to bid on it, even though he had no experience in running a ski resort. The Forest Service was pleased that Flint was interested in bidding on China Peak. They were confident that he could take on any task and be successful. He was just thirty-five when he signed the agreement with the Forest Service for a use permit to build China Peak, yet he was experienced beyond his years.

Flint formed the China Peak Corporation, with himself as president, and his long-time friend and partner in the helicopter companies, H.B. Armstrong, as the secretary-treasurer. He would put up 75% of the necessary capital, and Armstrong the other 25%. They would not require any stock to be sold, either public or private. The deal sounded almost too good to be true, and it was! On August 15, 1956, the contract was signed by Knute W. Flint and Leon Thomas, Sierra National Forest Supervisor, and work started that summer. A contract was soon signed with the Riblet Tramway Co. of Spokane, WA, to build the new chairlift. It was installed by Lowell Northrop Construction Co.; the total cost came to $150,000.

China Peak officially opened on January 18, 1958, with the new 5800 foot-long double chairlift, offering the intermediate and advanced skiers a ride of more than one mile. It climbed 1400 vertical feet to the summit of the volcanic outcropping, which is China Peak. Even the name of this mountain is attributed to Knute Flint, because originally it was Chinese Peak. It was changed in August of 1956 at Flint's request.

In addition to the chairlift, a Ford V-8 automobile engine powered a rope tow that pulled skiers to the base of Razorback. The outhouses that were located there commanded a magnificent mountain view. A small day lodge was built at the base of Chair #1. The old building housed the main office, ticket office and ski school near the base of Chair #1. Such refinements as food service and warm indoor restrooms would have to wait for another year or two. This beautiful little building was eventually torn down to make room for the present Day Lodge.

Chair #1 was the first chair to open, with loading at the base, and a loading and unloading station about two-thirds of the way up at Tower 12, at about 7800 feet elevation. The rider could unload here, or ride to the top and unload at 8500 feet. He could then ski down to Tower 12, reload, and ride back to the top, if snow conditions were sparse on the lower portion of the mountain.

The opening day crew included Boyd Turner, who had previously worked for the Lowell Northrup Company (the company that installed the chairlift). He served as the upper chair operator, and Jim Adams was the lower lift operator. Tommy Davis was in charge of parking and snow-plowing. Herb Schwartz was the first general manager, and Bud Nilsson was the Ski School Director.

Bud Nilsson was a 6'3" blond guy from Sweden, a friend of Stein Eriksson, and a phenomenal skier. Joe Weirick skied behind the two of them, and it was said you could not tell the difference, because they skied exactly the same. Bud was also a golf pro, and he had been teaching golf in Ligonier,

Pa., when he decided a little change of scenery was in order. He drove his red Thunderbird to California and settled in the Manhattan Beach area. He said the girls were pretty, and before he knew it he was a beach bum.

One day, one of his friends asked Bud if he would mind helping him and Vicky Hasher, the Kastle Ski distributor, unload a railroad car filled with skis. This is where he met Herb Schwartz, the new general manager of China Peak. When Herb learned that Bud was a Certified Ski Instructor and had been teaching in Sweden, he asked him if he would be interested in working at a new resort in the Sierra Mountains—China Peak. Bud drove up to the new resort and met with Knute Flint. He was offered the job as the first permanent Ski School Director. The job included room and board for the first season. This seemed like too good an offer to pass up, so Bud accepted. He moved into the lodge, and although it was unfinished, the bar and kitchen were in full operation. It was staffed with a chef, Andy Anderson, and a maitre' de, Pierre Ajoux, from France. The bar was considered very important.

The opening day dawned clear and cold, as the first skiers trudged into the loading line. With skis almost seven feet long, this was tough going. These skis were firmly strapped to the boot, with a spring steel cable that pushed the ski-boot into the toe piece. If that did not hold the boot firmly enough, a long leather strap called the Arlberg Strap, was wrapped around the ankle and fastened to the ski with a buckle. These bindings were not intended to release in a fall, as the releasable binding was still several years away. Falls were to be avoided at all costs, and a good wipe-out with bindings like these resulted in Tib-Fib fractures by the dozens. This type of binding and ski kept orthopedic surgeons busy all winter long, as these un-releasable bindings were very dangerous. Many old pictures of ski lodges had a skier or two with a leg in a cast, sitting in front of the fireplace.

That first season, snow packing and grooming was an unknown art. Skiing in unpacked snow with the equipment of the time was for the young, strong, and fool-hardy. It helped to bolster one's courage with a few beers. China Peak had fresh-fallen snow for their opening day, although it was delayed while the one and only lift was dug out enough to operate. China Peak had only one method for ski packing. It was done by dozens of skiers side-stepping up the hill in unison. This back-breaking task was rewarded by a free lift ticket for the day. Later, a contraption was invented to slightly improve on this method. A skier could ski downhill, towing a fifty-five gallon drum attached to a yoke. The skier could steer this rig just a little bit, but it was dangerous. Control was tricky. The skier had to be lucky as well as good to keep out of the way and avoid being run over.

Fashion has always played an important part in skiing. Wool pants were the in thing in 1958. Not the baggy tweeds of a few years ago, but pants that fit just a bit tighter. Warmth was a big factor, and these were the days when function defined form. Suspenders worked well with the wool pants; they were roomy enough for the wearer to be comfortable while exercising. The pants tapered below the knee to the ankle, and the bottoms were tucked into the low leather boot-top and held down with little stirrups under the foot. Brightly colored knitted wool sweaters were adorned with snowflakes and deer. Wool jackets and caps topped off the fashionable skier. The tighter stretch pants were a couple of years away.

Success seemed a distant dream on that opening day in 1958, and, in fact, it was a dream that Knute Flint would never achieve, in spite of his good intentions and months of hard work. Tons of money was poured into China Peak, and it would to be tough sledding for years to turn the resort into a money-making venture. An all-day lift ticket in 1958 was $5.00, and a room in the hotel was $6.00. From Los

Angeles, skiers could get a reservation by calling Dickens 2-7356. Skiers had one lift and about three different ways to ski down. The most popular run was Academy, but at the time, it was filled with tree stumps, narrow trails, and very rough terrain. The other runs were Beginner's Trail, Grouse, and Expert's Run. The promise of better trails and smoother runs in the future did little to soothe the sore feelings of the hardcore skier. The original runs were steep, narrow cat-tracks that crisscrossed the mountain. They were extremely hard to ski because there was not enough room to make safe turns. Skis got locked into deep ruts and they did the steering for you. The skier held on and hoped he could make that turn!

Money flowed out by the bucketfuls. During the second year, the Taylor-Wheeler Company, builders from Fresno, finished the hotel, restaurant, and bar. The fact that they were never paid for that building would have serious consequences in the future. That first winter, the remainder of the 1958–1959 season, China Peak operated on weekends only, and it was probably just as well, as there were many kinks to work out. The original plans, which were overly optimistic, called for a boat dock and marina at Huntington Lake. The China Peak Special Use Permit, consisting of 1300 acres, extended to the mouth of Big Creek, and then to the Huntington Lake shoreline. The summer of 1959 was spent improving trails and removing boulders to make the runs more skiable in light snow years.

Everyone was looking forward to the fall of 1959 and the year's first snowfall. Snow was late in coming that year, and in fact, China Peak was plagued by lack of snow for three of the first four years it was in operation. The season of 1959–1960 opened late, but with full daily operations. Jimmy Adams was in charge of Chair #1, Pete Azawedo was the lift operator, and Boyd Turner was Mountain Manager. Tommy Davis was in charge of parking and snow plowing, and Loran Martin, the postmaster from Huntington Lake, worked on weekends as the ticket seller. Joe and Joanne Senglaub joined the ski school staff, with Bud Nilsson as director. Herb Schwartz, the first General Manager, left and was replaced by Ed Seigel. Ed's wife, Lois, was an instructor. The ski school staff grew with weekend instructors Walt McMullen, Del LaFace, Norm Clark, George Kamienski, Tony Alfano, Tom Bottoms, and race coach Ray Kellner.

"We skied our butts off all day, and partied all night," Bud said to me. It must have been a great time. The bar played a prominent role in the social life of new China Peak employees. The new swimming pool was just a few steps outside of the bar, through French doors overlooking the pool area. Since the floor level of the bar was about six feet higher than the water level, a ski run was constructed from the bar to a jump, ending in the pool. Many a tipsy skier

Prior to 1990, the pool was a popular spot on summer days. It featured a full service bar, and restaurant service. The pool was filled in and cemented over during the summer of 1990. *Photo courtesy the Weirick collection.*

sobered up in a hurry, when the ice was too thin to hold his weight.

Also new for 1960 was a Doppelmayr T-bar lift. It was described in the 1959–1960 brochure:

"This easy-riding T-bar serves a long, wide beginner slope that is separated from the expert and intermediate areas. It rises 1,000 feet. Its location close to the lodge makes it an ideal place for younger children to ski while the family enjoys the upper slopes."

Eventually, this lift became famous as the first ski-lift in history to be repossessed.

The ski season of 1960–1961 was late in opening because of scant early snowfall. The following season, the weather pattern was reversed and China Peak was snowed in for five weekends. The resort lacked adequate snow-moving equipment to keep operational during winter storms. The resort did have one Tucker Sno Cat. This was an early version of a snow vehicle that had tracks on the rear end and skis on the front. It looked a bit like an army half-track from World War II. It was painted bright red and powered by a Ford V-8 engine. It traveled well on the snow, and by attaching a sheet of plywood between the front two skis, it could also do a fairly good job of packing ski trails. The name Sno Cat is the model name of the Tucker, but all grooming machines are later referred to as Snowcats.

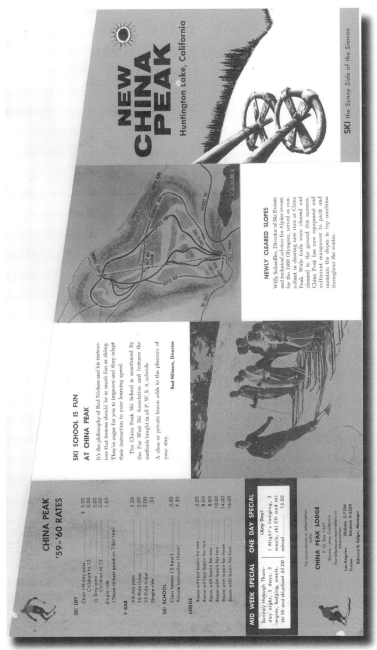

Printed for the 1959–1960 ski season. Please notice the prices and the only lift, Chair #1. There were several trails down, but none of them were easy.

This is the back of the first printed brochure of the new resort; it describes the new China Peak Lodge, the Riblet Chairlift, and the Doppelmayr T-Bar lift.

This is an early Sno-Cat. Although the name Sno-Cat is a Tucker vehicle, the common name for all packing machines now is "Snow Cat." China Peak's first over the snow vehicle was a Tucker with skis on the front end. Before snow machines were perfected, this type of vehicle did many different chores around ski resorts. *Photo courtesy the Rich Bailey collection.*

CHAPTER 3

A Problem of Money

By 1962, the proverbial wolf was barking at Flint's front door. However, if Flint was worried, he did well to cover it up. He had been busy in southern California with his other business ventures. He finally came up to China Peak for a short while, but did not stay permanently. When he left, his wife, Barbara, and Bud Nilsson became the resort managers.

The Forest Service was pressuring Flint to complete improvements to the sewage disposal facilities, do bridge repairs, improve electrical wiring, and do a general cleanup of the resort. Flint said he planned to borrow $5000 from friends to pay for the improvements, but creditors were forcing him closer and closer to bankruptcy. Creditors were getting anxious for their money, and were tired of his excuses.

On July 25, 1962, the *Fresno Bee* headline read: "Resort Operator Seeks Okay of Proposal for Debt Payoff." Knute's back was up against the wall, and he was running out of time. He wanted bankruptcy referee W.A. McGugin to allow him to continue operating, and more time to pay off debts. "We opened after a 32-year unbroken record of snow, and then experienced the worst snow drought ever experienced in this area of the Sierra," he pleaded. "This was followed by such a heavy snowfall this year; we were snowed out for five weekends in February."

The referee agreed, and set up another meeting for August 15, 1962. By this time, the *Fresno Bee* reported on August 16, 1962, "Plan Is Sought To Pay Debts of China Peak." Federal Bankruptcy Referee W.A. McGugin appointed a three-man creditor's committee to advise on the operation of the China Peak Corporation, until a decision was made on the corporation's request for approval on a plan to pay off debt, which by then amounted to $1,263,572. The committee consisted of Raymond Kellner, representing Kellner Lumber Company, which built the employee's dormitory, Jack Pieroni of Mid-Valley Sports Center, and Donald Hicks, of Pittsburgh-Des Moines Steel Company. On September 11, 1962, *The Fresno Bee* reported:

Ski Resort Will Stay Open in Attempt to Pay Debts. McGugin also will hear and decide on a counter claim filed by Flint against the Kellner Lumber Company in connection with a dormitory at the resort which collapsed under heavy snows.

China Peak, Knute Flint, and his creditors were side-slipping down a dangerous slope, a slope from which they would never recover.

Flint was ordered to explain how he would pay off his debt. He listed $128,000 in assets, including $3000 in cash, and the same amount in motor vehicles. The corporation's debts included $865,857 in unsecured claims, $364,715 in secured claims, $17,000 in back taxes, and $16,000 in fees to the federal government. The secured claims were on the chairlift, the lodge, a power plant, first aid building, ski shop, swimming pool, and other equipment. It was obvious to even the casual observer that it would take a lot of lift tickets at $5.00 each to pay off debts of over one million dollars.

Ski resorts, like farming, face boom and bust years, depending heavily on weather. For a ski resort, ideally, storms will come during the week, and weekends would be clear, cold, and welcoming to skiers. Roads and parking lots would be plowed, walkways and ticket lines would be shoveled, and everything would be ready to operate. This was an ideal situation, and it rarely happened. Storms that occurred on busy weekends caused huge traffic jams, frayed nerves, and lost money for the resort. For the resort to be snowed in for five weekends was indeed very unfortunate, and it would be difficult to recover from. Proper snow-moving equipment and crew training would have given China Peak much needed revenue during the peak season. Many of the essential resort workers lived in Shaver Lake and Auberry, and were unable to get to work. Even with full manpower, the proper equipment was not available.

Restrooms were in short supply in the early years. There were some in the hotel, but the hillside restrooms were located partway up the mountain. You could stop in on your way down, but going up to them was difficult. In order to visit the restrooms and load onto Chair #1, the new T-bar lift was installed to take skiers and beginners part way up the hill. This helped to get skiers out of the base area, and it was well used. The restrooms also operated on the septic tank principle, and the Forest Service was forcing Flint to install a sewage treatment system. This was just one of the required improvements he did not have the money to pay for.

Unfortunately, Flint never got around to paying for the new T-bar lift, and one summer day, the company that installed it came in and backed their trucks into the parking lot. They moved in with cutting torches, cut down the towers, and hauled the whole lift away. I don't think I have ever heard of another ski lift ever being repossessed. It was later sold to Monmoth College in Colorado. Dealing with Flint, one had to be resourceful.

A front page article in the *Fresno Bee* on April 16, 1964, spreads the bad news. The resort's financial condition was announced to the public.

Referee Finds Ski Resort Firm Bankrupt

Federal Bankruptcy Referee William A. McGugin made the decision after Flint said he did not have the $45,000 to deposit *on his debt, as ordered by the court in October. Since 1962, he had been unable to make payments on the original debt. The decision ended two years of hearings. Flint first filed papers in 1962 asking for more time in which to pay off his original debt of $1,263,572. In October of 1963, McGugin put attorney Max Hayden in charge of the resort, but Hayden left Flint as manager for the remainder of the ski season. McGugin said he did not believe the law would allow any more extensions, and declared the corporation bankrupt.*

Attorney Kendall Manock, representing the creditor's committee, asked for a bankruptcy declaration and the sale of the property. Some of the creditors had also asked that the resort be sold to Dave McCoy, operator of Mammoth Mountain. McCoy was interested in acquiring the resort, and made a very good offer. The creditors were tired of waiting, and filed an affidavit in federal court, asking for McGugin's removal as referee, contending that he had already given Flint too much time.

China Peak Resort Will Be Put Up For Sale

The *Fresno Bee* reported on June 7, 1964, that Federal Judge M.D. Crocker had granted a motion to sell the ski resort, free of liens. Max Hayden, who was appointed trustee after its President, Knute Flint, was unable to make the resort on a money making business. Negotiations were expected to start soon, and Dave McCoy was ready to put his money on the table.

SKIING INTO THE SIXTIES

During the early 1960s, skiing became the fastest growing sport in America. The overwhelming success of the 1960 Winter Olympics brought new interest in skiing to California. This was the first time the Olympics had been

This is what greeted the skier on his first ride of the day on old Chair #1, before the new triple Chair #1 was installed. Lift capacity out of the base area has been a problem since day one, but it has sure improved since this photo was taken. Weekend crowds always caused lines to back up, but soon everybody will get out of the base, and heading to other runs and other lifts. *Photo courtesy Pete Scaparo collection.*

broadcast on television, and many new people were attracted to the sport. Alex Cushing's Squaw Valley was now known world-wide, and the west was becoming known for its world class skiers, and for the Sierra Nevada Mountains. Dave McCoy's Mammoth Mountain was hosting record numbers of skier visits. Badger Pass in Yosemite was also showing large increases in skiers.

China Peak had the easiest highway access. It had outstanding terrain and fine snow, yet it was unable to grow because it had yet to make its first dollar in profit. It is easy to be objective in 2008 and look back to 1964 to find reasons the resort failed. But the outstanding reason had to be lack of capital. With the boom of interest in skiing, the resort should have been a natural, yet with only one chair lift, skiers piled up at the bottom. When they finally got their turn to ride to the top, they were greeted with ungroomed snow, stumps, moguls, narrow runs, and tough skiing. Many of the skiers of the day were new to the sport and found the learning curve intimidating and dangerous. Not everybody was tough enough to stick it out. Skiing was here to stay, but customers demanded better conditions than China Peak had to offer.

Skis, bindings, clothing, and everything related to skiing were improving. The old "bear trap" bindings that connected boots to skis with an iron grip had given way to the new releasable binding that allowed the foot to separate from the ski during a twisting fall. The Arlberg Strap that held the foot down had been replaced by the safety strap, allowing the foot to move independently from the ski when it separated. Leather boots that stopped at the ankle were being replaced by plastic boots that came halfway up the calf. Boot-top tibia fractures were becoming fewer, but still occurred. Although the 1960 equipment was increasing skiing safety, there was still much room for improvement. A ski that released in a fall was dragged along behind the skier, still connected to the foot by the safety strap. Oftentimes, this ski thrashed about in

Modern day skiers may just recognize the boulder in the foreground. All efforts to remove it when the building was expanded failed, so it remained in place. It now extends into the locker area, under the Day Lodge. (This photo was taken from the old Chair One, looking down and back.)

windmill fashion, being dragged behind a sliding skier. Cuts to the head and face were too often the result. The resorts required the use of the safety strap to keep skis from plunging downhill when a skier fell and his ski separated.

The hot skis for the 1960s would have to include the new Head Standards. In 1950, Howard Head, a Harvard graduate with an engineering degree, developed, designed, manufactured, and marketed the first metal laminate skis. These skis were made of two layers of aluminum bonded around a core of plywood at a very high pressure; the outer layer made of plastic. By 1952, Head introduced skis with tempered steel edges. His skis were lighter and faster than the old wood skis and earned the name "cheaters" because they were easier to ski. Gradually, better equipment was coming on the market, and the ski industry was growing by leaps and bounds. Ski-brakes were invented to keep skis from plummeting downhill after separating in a fall, but even after they were perfected and proven safe, the resorts were slow to change. For several years, they required both safety straps and brakes.

China Peak would have to improve their facilities if they were to survive. Flint had grand plans for his area—not just as a ski resort, but functioning as a year-round vacation spot, including a marina at the lake, and a large hotel near the top of the mountain. He envisioned connecting these resorts with a small train. This may have been overly optimistic, but an abandoned railroad existed, a remnant from the logging history of the area.

Flint had the foresight to get the resort started, but keeping it growing was a monumental task. The basics were in place. The valuable land agreement with the Sierra National Forest was worth its weight in gold. Little did the owners know that there would probably be no more permits granted in the Sierra. China Peak was on a main state highway, with easy access. Skiing was becoming such an important winter sport that the highway department was starting to provide better snow removal. The city of Fresno was contributing the bulk of skiers. The foggy, dreary, dampness of the San Joaquin valley winters stirred the need to escape to the mountains. Bosses' telephones were ringing off the walls with employees calling in sick, taking vacation days, and just plain taking days off to ski.

Flint's management skills that were touted so much in the beginning were now starting to be stretched too thin. His successful helicopter business was suffering, and China Peak was not breaking even, let alone showing a profit. Flint himself was absent much of the time. He may have been tending to his other business interests, or he may have, as many speculated, felt the grass was greener on the other side of the mountain.

CHAPTER 4

The Weirick Years

The Weirick name is a familiar family name in Fresno. J.R. Weirick was a well-respected businessman. He was the founder of Midland Savings, and a graduate of Fresno State. J.R. had attended Fresno State when they had summer sessions at Huntington Lake, and he formed a great affinity with the area from his hiking and swimming. The love of the mountains was passed on to his daughter, Geraldine, born in 1935, and son, Joseph Benson Weirick, born in 1938.

Joe Benson is a native Fresnan, a graduate of Fresno High School and Fresno State, majoring in Business, earning his degree in 1960. J.R. had a place for young Joe at Midland Savings; he started as a teller and worked at every position to gain business savvy. Joe's education and experience did not go unnoticed, and his father made him a loan officer at age twenty-five, which was quite an accomplishment. That experience would pay great dividends in a very different environment in the not-too-distant future.

Joe had the youth, stamina, and, above all, the education in business to turn the ski area around. Joe had learned to ski at Yosemite's Badger Pass Ski School under the direction of the legendary Luggi Foeger. Nic Fiore had not arrived yet; he came in 1957. Joe's older sister was a good skier, and he couldn't let her beat him. He had to keep up with her.

Joe began skiing at China Peak while he was in college. He loved skiing and had considered investing in it, as he could see the problems Flint was having. Joe recognized that Flint's shortage of capital was a major factor. The two Weiricks, Joe and J.R., talked about investing in the resort many times. Joe

Joe Weirick is demonstrating near perfect form and the hottest equipment of the sixties: Vuarnet shades, leather gloves, leather buckle-boots, and the famous Arlberg strap to hold the boot firmly to the ski. This type of binding was very dangerous and resulted in many leg injuries. It was replaced later by much safer bindings and ski brakes that stopped skis from running away downhill after releasing during a fall. *Photo courtesy the Weirick collection.*

was in favor of buying China Peak, but J.R., being older and wiser, advised him against it. J.R. did not want to get involved with Flint. The ski area was on Forest Service land so there was no first trust deed. J.R. felt that if they waited long enough, they could get it without assuming the debts it had incurred. Flint's problems continued to worsen as the creditors were threatening to take over the resort and liquidate the assets.

In August of that year, Federal Bankruptcy Referee W.A. McGugin appointed a three-man creditor's committee to advise on the operation of the ski resort until a decision could be made on the corporation's request for a plan to pay off the debts. This committee consisted of Ray Kellner, Jack Pieroni, and Donald Hicks. (Kellner represented The Kellner Lumber Company, Pieroni was from Mid-Valley Sports Center, and Hicks represented Pittsburg-Des Moines Steel.)

The *Fresno Bee*, August 16, 1962, reported:

McGugin also will hear and decide on a counter claim filed by Flint against the Kellner Lumber Company in connection with a dormitory at the resort which collapsed under heavy snows.

The *Fresno Bee*, October 16, 1963, reported:

Flint Gets Okay for Ski Lodge Operation.

Knute Flint, president of the China Peak Corporation, was given permission to operate the resort until April 15, 1964, at a bankruptcy hearing, yesterday.

"I still have confidence that China Peak will be a major ski resort, some day," said Mr. Flint. He was speculating of course, but truer words were never spoken. Flint listed his assets at $128,000, and his debts at $1,263,572, and this was not a very good ratio in any business. On October 20th, 1963,

Bankruptcy Referee McGugin reversed his earlier decision, and decided to appoint Fresno attorney Max Hayden in control of China Peak and decide its fate. Joe and J.R. Weirick were waiting and watching. They knew patience would pay off if they just let the scenario play out. Their timing proved to be perfect.

Federal Judge M.D. Crocker granted a motion on June 7, 1964, to sell the resort, with attorney Max Hayden appointed as trustee. The decision was made to sell the resort free of liens, since it was located on federal land, and liens could not be transferred. Taylor-Wheeler Builders of Fresno was the only bidder and bought the property for $157,022.16. They still had not been paid for the hotel, and just wanted to protect their investment.

It was now time for the Weiricks to make their move. They could pay Taylor-Wheeler a small profit, and in return, convince them to sell China Peak debt-free.

On September 15, 1964, the *Fresno Bee* cried out the news, if somewhat inaccurately:

Fresno, Mammoth Interests Buy China Peak Ski Resort.

The reality was that the resort was purchased by Weirick and Company of Fresno from Taylor-Wheeler Builders of Fresno, the builders of the hotel. Weirick and Company took the resort off their hands for just a small amount more than Taylor-Wheeler's $157,022.16 bid. The exact purchase price was never disclosed; however, reports indicate it was less than $200,000. Taylor-Wheeler had no interest in running a ski resort; they just wanted to recoup some of the money that was owed to them for building the hotel.

The acquisition of China Peak occurred just days before Joe's twenty-sixth birthday in 1964. Joe was young, eager, and he had talent. He was ready for the biggest challenge of his life so far. He was ready and willing to build a ski resort out of its many bits and pieces. The assets were there, but were hardly more that the bare-bones of a ski resort. The most important asset was the Land Use Permit with the Sierra National Forest. That would be the last permit issued for a ski resort in the area. The first chair lift, Chair #1, was in and operating, but it was in need of much maintenance. This was not the only issue. There were many other problems, from initial design to poor upkeep. The operation suffered from lack of good management, insufficient capital, and not enough skiers. The irregular snowfall just made matters worse. Joe Weirick was eager to start, and he was ready to build a bigger and better resort than Badger Pass.

THE START OF A NEW RESORT

The deal was in the works, but to Joe it seemed to be taking forever, as attorney Robert G. Carter and the Weiricks struggled with the endless details of liens, law suits, and accounts payable. Joe finally decided to take a vacation, and set sail for the warm waters of the South Pacific with some of his friends. He was sitting on the deck of a sailboat in Tahiti when he got the news that his father was trying to reach him. When he finally found a telephone and called his father, he got the good news. His father told him that the deal had gone through. He called this his twenty-sixth birthday gift. Joe wasted no time in rushing home to see just exactly what they had bought. The list of things that were lacking, and of things that were needed, seemed to be endless.

Perhaps it would be better just to concentrate on the good points. It had location, and everybody knew that location was everything. At the time, there were prospects of a new ski development in the Mineral King area of Sequoia-Kings Canyon, but it was unsure whether it would ever be developed. The Disney Corporation was the most likely developer, but the decision had been postponed indefinitely. If it were to be approved, it would likely be quite some time before it would be workable, because no roads existed in the area. As time would prove, the Mineral King area would never be developed into a ski resort. This lack of a competing resort within driving distance of Fresno made China Peak all the more attractive. It was time to roll up the proverbial sleeves and fix what needed to be fixed to make China Peak a world class resort. Joe wasted no time in getting started.

Knute Flint obviously left much to be desired in the management department. He had other business interests, and was present at China Peak only part time. (He often left his wife, Barbara, in charge.) His first general manager, Herb Schwartz, lasted only one season, and he didn't stay at the resort for the entire winter. He had an import-export business in the Los Angeles area and he wanted to be there part of the time. He was replaced the second season by Ed Siegel. Ed's wife, Lois, was a ski instructor, and worked for Bud Nilsson in the ski school. The Siegels soon tired of the situation and left the following season for Sugar Bowl. This gives some insight to the condition that Joe Weirick found his new business. It was going to take a clean sweep to get the resort in order, and there were times Joe and J.R. questioned themselves as to whether they had made the right decision. Only time would prove them right or wrong.

Escrow closed on the resort in September of 1964, and when Joe walked into China Peak Ski Resort on his first day as owner, he paused, looked around, probably scratched his head and wondered, *where do we start?*

Joe Weirick was a businessman, and a very young businessman at that. Until 1964, his only business experience was with savings and loan industry. Very wisely, he chose Don Redmond to be vice president and resort manager. Don was forty-one years old when he came to China Peak, and he had been general manager at Mammoth for the last eight years. He had been affiliated with Mammoth owner/developer Dave McCoy for the last seventeen years and had gained valuable experience. Don also brought in Bob Autry, a thirty-one-year-old certified ski instructor from Mammoth, to lead the China Peak ski school. Joe was putting together a very good management team, which he was going to need.

The Winter Olympics in Squaw Valley in 1960 did much to elevate the California ski scene. For the first time, television carried many of the events into our living rooms. President Richard Nixon opened the games. The world watched as Californian Andrea Mead Lawrence skied down Papoose to hand the Olympic Torch to Kenneth Henry so he could light the Olympic flame. Jean Vuarnet became the first ski racer to win on metal skis.

Clothing had made some huge changes, and the U.S. team had stretch fabric pants for the first time. Ski clothes were starting to evolve into a much more skier-friendly design, with even more innovation to come in the near future. Skiers were still burdened with lacing up leather boots, but buckle boots were just over the horizon. Looking back, one can't help but wonder why someone didn't think of things like that sooner.

The Volkswagen Beetle was the skier's favorite ride. With the engine located over the rear axle, it handled snow-covered roads beautifully. The car had the neatest little rack that carried skis safely with the tails pointed down, near the rear bumper, and the tips over the rear window at a most jaunty angle. Corvairs were also hot items, but they never surpassed the faithful bug. Volkswagen heaters worked perfectly on the long uphill pulls, but provided only cool air on the downgrade, as the engine cooled. The VW bus was good for camping at parking lots, but they were so slow on the trip uphill.

REBUILDING CHINA PEAK

China Peak had a long way to go if it was ever to become the world class resort that Knute Flint envisioned. The first and most important item on the list was improving the restroom facilities. The Forest Service would not issue Weirick and

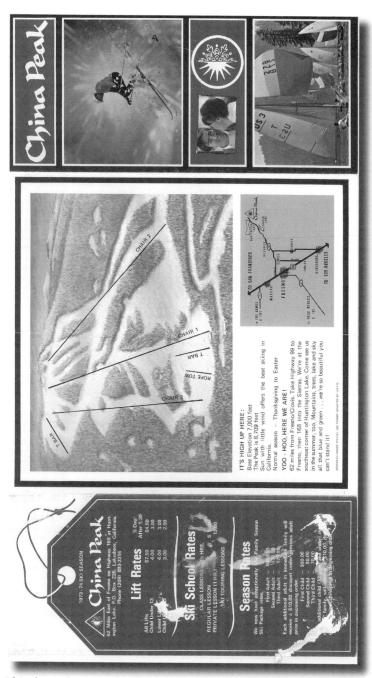

This shows the prices for the season, $7.50 for the lift ticket. Notice the map, it shows the new lift at Firebowl and the rope tow in the beginner area.

Company, Inc., a permit to operate until they removed all the septic tanks from their property and installed an approved sewage system. This seemed like an insurmountable problem, especially if the resort was to operate the winter of '64–'65. Joe was fortunate in locating the components for an approved sewage treatment system in Fresno, and with the help of his new staff he had the system installed and running in time to open at first snowfall.

Joe's team, in addition to newcomers Don Redmon and Bob Autry, also had some holdovers from Flint's days. Otto Tamm had been Ski School Director after Nilsson left, and he would now devote his time to ski patrol, which was his first love. The Forest Service required a ski school with a certified instructor as director, and Otto was qualified. Otto had been a member of Fresno Ski Patrol since 1958. (Otto's story is a unique chapter within itself, and it is too important to cover in brief. He will be covered in detail separately.)

Joanne Senglaub, another certified ski instructor, stayed on from Flint's team. She had worked at China Peak as an instructor, but left to go back to Mammoth during the bankruptcy. She will play an important part in the future of not only China Peak, but much more. Tall, tan, and beautiful, a charming smile, and a vivacious personality, all added to her superb skiing ability, and defined Joanne. She liked the Shaver Lake community, and during the years she worked for Flint she bought a small cabin near the village. In the early sixties, China Peak suffered some very lean years when they were unable to stay open full-time, even during the season. Joanne and many of the other employees took whatever work was available; she did waitressing, house cleaning, and even took in ironing.

Much of the work started as soon as escrow closed in September, 1964, transferring the ownership to the Weirick Company. Joe Weirick and Don Redmon had a crew ranging from twenty-seven to thirty-five workers, and four bulldozers working full-time, twelve hours a day, changing China Peak from a good mountain to a superb one. The ambitious building program also included rebuilding the dormitory which had collapsed under the snow load two winters earlier. It was used to house employees and guests. The main lodge dining room was enlarged, and an expanded ski rental area was built. A new and wider bridge was built over Big Creek to make it easier to walk from the lodge to the lifts. Footings

Joanne was an integral part of management with her husband Joe. She was an excellent skier, an outstanding instructor, and continued teaching well into the Sierra Summit years, long after she and her husband had sold the resort. *Photo courtesy the Weirick collection.*

were poured for a new T-bar to serve beginner areas, with hopes the machinery would arrive before the first snowfall.

Snow came early in the fall of 1964. It was a good omen for the first year of China Peak under the ownership of Joe Weirick and his very capable team. By Thanksgiving, there was five feet of packed snow at the bottom and ten feet at the top of the mountain. Opening day for 1964 was the Friday before Thanksgiving. The next day, the one and only lift broke down.

Boyd Turner heard about the lift breaking down as he was driving down Highway 99. He called Joe to offer his expertise. He knew the machinery very well because he had helped install it and he was its first operator. Boyd had worked for Flint at China Peak, but left for more steady work in the construction industry.

When Joe explained the breakdown to Boyd, he knew just what to do. It needed a new bearing that would have to be manufactured. With strong team spirit and much determination, the new part was manufactured overnight by Valley Foundry in Fresno and installed the following day by Boyd and his mechanics. By eight o'clock Sunday morning, the lift was up and running. Joe hired Boyd back on the China Peak team right on the spot, and he stayed with the resort for many years. People and events like this helped form the cohesive bond that made China Peak grow.

The first season under Joe and Don, the winter of '64–'65, was a success. Skiing continued until May first, and a total of 22,000 lift tickets were sold at a price of $6.00, up from the original $5.00. Hotel rooms cost $10.00, and the twelve rooms in the new addition were the first to have bathrooms; the original hotel rooms had only a wash basin, with the showers and toilets down at the end of the hall. Guests could reserve rooms from Los Angeles by calling DIckens 2-7365 or in Fresno by dialing BAldwin 9-3224.

The summer of 1965 gave added enthusiasm to the young ski area. Projects left unfinished when the snow began to fall were now being completed and spirits were running high. China Peak was moving toward a more solid footing. The runs were being widened and the rocks were being removed to eliminate hazards. Many of the runs named by Flint had no meaning to local people. One was Kamboli Bowl, and no one even knew what that meant. Joe and his father changed many of the names to represent the area, like Huntington,

Joe and Joanne Weirick, owners of China Peak, dressed for the big Halloween party in the late 1960s, reflected the light-hearted atmosphere of the time. *Photo courtesy the Weirick collection.*

Tollhouse, and Academy. Other runs kept their original names, like Fire Bowl and Razorback. Fire Bowl got its name after a fire started when timber was being taken out to build a beginner slope. Academy and other beginner runs were groomed and contoured. Work was also progressing at the base area, with general cleaning and painting.

Joe and Joanne were married in the fall of 1964. The husband-wife team proved to be unbeatable. Joanne continued as a very popular ski instructor and played a valuable role in management.

Plans were in the works to add another lift, Chair #2, which started near Highway 168 and unloaded near the very top of the mountain, within sight of the top of Chair #1. China Peak had very poor ski run access from the base area, and hopefully Chair #2 would alleviate this problem. Some experts questioned the choice of location for this lift's bottom loading area, but it was installed as designed.

WINTER, 1966

By opening day of 1966, Chair #2 was up and running. As time will show, it would have been better to have located it nearer the new Day Lodge. The cafeteria was open, and with it, the brand new and very popular sun-deck. There were new restrooms in the Day Lodge, and the rental area was enlarged. The hotel featured a dining room, a cocktail lounge, and a complete sports shop. A single-room rate was $8.00; however, that was without a bathroom. If you wanted that added convenience, you would have to shell out a whopping $12.00.

Skiing was becoming an accepted family sport. The new and improved runs made skiing much easier for the beginner and intermediate skier. It became more apparent that the easier it was to ski the mountain, the more enjoyable it was for everybody, pointing to the need for good instructors and a good ski school.

This early photograph shows the Day Lodge and sundeck. Notice that the beginner slopes had not yet been re-graded to slope to the east. The original grade ended just in front of the Day Lodge, and more than one novice skier ended his run with a collision into the building. *Photo courtesy the Weirick collection.*

China Peak's racing team, under the coaching of Ray Kellner, Otto Tamm, Stan Beach, and Bob Autry was improving each year. China Peak has had a strong history of producing outstanding young racers. The Tamm sisters, Kati and Tiina, and Janet Turner, were among the best.

On March 28, 1966, the *Fresno Bee* reported:

The Walt Disney organization has been given the green light to develop Mineral King. Disney had been the successful bidder in 1965, when the bids were opened at the Porterville office of the Sequoia National Forest.

Would the skiing public be faithful to China Peak, or would they desert the resort that Joe Weirick and his staff had worked so hard to groom to perfection?

A new resort at Mineral King appeared to be a sure thing: Yes, many problems had to be solved, but with Disney's bottomless pockets, no problems were insurmountable. The powerful Sierra Club had approved the recreational development in March, 1965, so it seemed that any and all problems could be addressed. The Forest Service had many restrictions to protect the secluded spot where the best skiing would be found, and no roads existed into the area. The Disney Organization had even proposed a monorail into their new proposed ski area to protect the wilderness. The Sierra Club, however, reversed their decision in May, 1965, and voted to oppose Disney's development, labeling it another "Disneyland." In June, 1969, the Sierra Club filed suit against the resort project. Eventually, the Disney plans were dropped, and in January of 1978, President Jimmy Carter merged the Mineral King area into Sequoia National Park, and the prospects for a ski development ended. China Peak would remain the last resort to be built in the Sierra Nevada range.

After the Winter Olympics were held in Squaw Valley, many predicted that a ski boom would follow, but those predictions proved to be overly optimistic. The ski population did not increase very significantly during the mid-sixties; however, by 1968 and 1969, skiing was really starting to take off. Equipment was getting better all the time. The wooden skis were being replaced by metal and composites. Boots were easier to put on and take off. China Peak had expanded parking and added more restrooms and lockers. Each of these improvements added to the enjoyment of the ski day. More and more families were coming into the sport, and the amenities became more family friendly.

The winter of 1968 saw the opening of Fire Bowl, with a new T-bar lift to pull skiers to the top. This gorgeous bowl is within sight of the unloading areas of both Chairs #1 and it was easily accessed from this lift. Fire Bowl was the original name given by Knute Flint, and it was so named because a fire started there as timber was being harvested from the runs. Easy intermediate skiing and wonderful views make this bowl a favorite with many skiers. Snow piles up here and the runs are in the shade on springtime afternoons, keeping the snow firm.

The gentle skiing made this a favorite run for instructors to bring their intermediate classes. Students could ski all the way down to the lodge from Fire Bowl, by way of Academy, giving them a run of about two and a half miles. This was a very impressive run, and most beginning skiers who take lessons could do it easily and safely on their very first day. Novices were always in a hurry to get out of the base area and get away from those rope tows, and they looked forward to seeing a new part of the mountain. The rope tow in the base area at that time was powered by a trusty Ford V-8 sixty horsepower automobile engine, and the downhill ropes were supported by old car wheels hung from poles and trees.

This simple but somewhat temperamental system earned its keep for many years, towing beginners up the bunny hills. The leather gloves that skiers wore then would soon became soaked from grabbing the wet rope and hanging on for dear life, as the rope pulled the skier uphill. The uphill rope coasted along in the snow until the skier picked it up for the trip up the hill. A new T-bar tow was built in 1965 to replace the earlier lift that was repossessed when Flint owned the resort. This new tow was a welcome improvement. When we look back at the hardships and struggles to learn to ski, it's easy to see why many beginners lost interest early.

JANUARY, 1969

The winter of 1969 delivered snow, snow, and more snow. On January 19, 1969, the *Fresno Bee* reported,

Avalanche Curtails China Peak Skiing. An avalanche of wet snow tumbled from the Face stacking up 14 feet of crumbled

snow on a lower trail, Academy. Fortunately it occurred early in the morning before skiers were on the slopes, reported Joanne Weirick.

What Joanne did not report was that Joe and Boyd Turner had triggered the avalanche with their new avalanche control cannon. They still had a bit to learn about the control of an avalanche.

The heavy winter snows continued during January, closing down China Peak Chairs #1 and #2. By January 30, Chair #1 resumed operation after being shut down for

Joe Weirick contemplating the heavy drifts of the winter that buried a California Division of Highways snowplow. Highway 168 was closed for several days, stranding many guests at the hotel. The kitchen and bar were fully stocked and nobody asked for a refund. The storm dumped twenty feet of snow at the base, and thirty feet at the top of Chair #1. This storm still holds the record for the most snow in China Peak-Sierra Summit history.
Photo courtesy the Weirick collection.

twelve days, and work turned to digging out Chair #2. Manager Joe Weirick had his problems, as fifteen feet of snow buried the unloading ramp of Chair #2. More storms followed, and by mid-February, China Peak had thirty guests stranded at the hotel. The hotel was well prepared, with plenty of food and a well-stocked bar, so nobody complained. They were warm and well-fed, and had perfect excuses for not being at work. The highway was closed by the heavy snows for twenty-six days. A Division of Highways motor grader was buried for two days while working to open the road. Thirty-foot snow banks on either side of the road had collapsed near Tamarack Pass, and briefly trapped the operator. Joe Weirick and his avalanche team came to the rescue with dynamite, and blasted out a path for the machine.

By the next day, the highway was cleared enough that all the guests were able to drive out. There have been heavy snow storms in subsequent years, but the old-timers will always remember the winter of 1969. There have been heavy snow years and light snow years, yet that winter stands alone, since no year has ever matched that famous winter of 1969. The resort remained open every day; as Boyd Turner said, "Joe wouldn't have it any other way."

The two chairlifts operating at full speed kept skiers moving, and helped with the traffic jams at the base area. The loading station at Chair #2 was not accessible from the base, unless the skier first rode up the hill on Chair #1, and skied down to load on Chair #2 for his next ride, so it was still difficult to get out of the base area for that first run. A new lift was needed from the base, and in 1972, Chair #3 was added. It loaded from the base area near the creek, and terminated near the summit of China Peak. By now, skiers were being moved out of the base area more efficiently.

CHAPTER 5

Skiing into the Seventies

The skiing public was growing now at a steady pace. China Peak continued to grow, making improvements and providing better skiing for their customers. Skiers were becoming more sophisticated in their expectations. They wanted good runs, adequate lift capacity, and good food. The trends of the times were changing, and the skier's clothes were becoming more informal. The ski resorts were seeing the effect of the counter-culture. The style was a holdover from the sixties: tie-dyes and bell bottoms fit right in with longer hair, beards, and sideburns. About the only functional good that we can say about wearing jeans to ski is that they didn't cost much. The bottoms got soaking wet, and soon froze. Leather boots were just about gone from the scene, as they were soon relinquished to back tables at yard sales. Plastic and composite boots were the in thing, in terrible outlandish colors, no less. Who can forget the Scott boot, with the hinge near the sole, and the front and back moving apart, to let the foot enter? They were comfortable and easy to slip on, but they were certainly lacking in control. The foot fit so loosely in the boot that when the skier rotated a foot to turn the ski, the message to turn left the foot but never reached the ski.

China Peak suffered from inadequate lift capacity to move skiers from the Day Lodge, where most people changed into their ski-clothes and boots, to the tops of the mountains where the runs started. The problem had existed since the early days of the resort's existence, and Chair #2 helped the problem, but never completely alleviated it.

The skiers are following ski school director Phil Kerridge (in the lighter jacket). Close behind Phil in perfect formation are Scott McLagan, George and Melanie Kinney, Skip Bullock, Dan Clack, Alan Bertrand and Denys Liboz. The Chinese characters can be very loosely translated to mean "China Peak". This beautiful piece of art debuted in time for the 1969–1970 ski season.

Chair #3 was built and installed by mid-December, 1973. It was ready for operation for the Christmas holidays. This new chair starts close by the creek and terminates near the peak, with an intermediate unloading ramp about three-fourths of the way to the top. By unloading here, skiers ski to the top of

Express. They can stay on the chair and ride to the top unloading terminal, exit, and ski Big Creek, Dynamite, or Express.

Some things were out of the management's control during that busy season; the lack of snow, and the Arab oil embargo of 1974 are two examples. President Jimmy Carter set the national highway speed limit at 55 MPH to save gasoline. Do any of us remember the long lines at the gas stations? How can we forget?

Skiing had grown at about 10% per year since the 1950s, with a spike in 1962 due to the Olympics, but growth had tapered off during the 1970s. China Peak needed more guests, and it would be nice to have them in the summer to replace the skiers. Perhaps more guests could be enticed to visit with the right entertainment. A local version of a rock festival might just be the thing, and so the idea for "China Sun" was born.

Mountain Press, August 29, 1977. Mike O'Halloran reported:

> *The best and most professionally produced event in the mountains," is the way Don Bean of China Peak describes the upcoming China Sun.*
>
> *This is not going to be a rock concert; it's going to be an event in the mountains for everyone." According to Bean, "There will be a large variety of booths with all manner of artisans. There will be merchants displaying sporting goods, four-wheel drive vehicles, and demonstrations in stunt skiing by a professional acrobatic team just back from a tour in South America. All this is in addition to music by Pablo Cruise and Danny O'Keefe.*

On September 4, the big day arrived and 5000 people attended. Many attendees drove up just to escape the heat of late summer in the valley. The day was bright and sunny; the guests relaxed on picnic blankets and lawn chairs, with a cold beer in hand. In addition to having a good time, many returned home sunburned and tired. The day was a grand success, and Joe Weirick and his staff had proven that China Peak could be year-round resort and could attract visitors in the summer as well as winter.

THE BEGINNING OF SNOWMAKING

By November 25, the first storm of the 1977 winter season hit the Sierra, giving hope that the drought of the last few years may have come to an early end. That small storm, however, did not end the drought, and the lack of snow meant no skiing. That translated to no income for China Peak. Joe and his team had been busy planning for dry seasons. Joe made the decision to commit a large investment in a costly new concept that was being used at some other resorts. That concept was snowmaking. Joe had experimented with snowmaking on a small scale, using a fan attached to a garden hose to spray snow around sparse areas, but the need there was for a much larger snowmaking effort. This monumental event was big news for China Peak skiers, and received news coverage in the local paper.

The *Fresno Bee*, December 6, 1977. Gene Rose reported:

China Peak's Man Made Snow

It snowed in the Sierra, last night. Despite the cloudless skies and a lack of storms, snow fell on a three or four acre section of the Sierra, even though no storms had been predicted for the mountain area east of Fresno. It was man made snow, shot out of a space age cannon with many of the sights and sounds of a rocket launch.

The snow was produced by a snow making machine, which the China Peak ski area hopes to beat Mother Nature's reluctance to do what has become more and more difficult to do, SNOW.

The $40,000 machine utilizes water from a nearby river, (actually Big Creek), pumped to the machine which is presently being used in an attempt to blanket a 20 acre site on the lower slopes.

Weirick said he hopes to be able to open the area to "limited skiing" on Friday at the area served by a T-bar.

This "toe in the water" testing of the expensive concept of snowmaking was just the first step in what was to become a very extensive system years later. The machine that the newspaper article mentioned is a Hedco, which was primarily a big blower, and sprayed a mixture of water and air into the sub-freezing sky to produce snow. China Peak was the first in our area of California to use man-made snow.

THE END OF THE WEIRICK CHAPTER

As the seventies were winding down, so were the wonderful laid-back years of the Weiricks, Joe and Joanne. They had had a good ride: they took a bare-bones ski resort and built it into a beautiful, productive ski area. All had not been accomplished that needed to be to make this a finished product, but one does not make excuses for the progress. They had invested long hard hours and much money. They had plenty of worries and much, much hard work. They had good help and faithful employees that stuck by them through thick and thin. The Weirick name is just as permanent as the name, China Peak. The two are synonymous, interchangeable, and a permanent part of our Shaver Lake community.

There are new owners waiting in the wings, willing to try their hand at running a ski resort. The new people are not at all experienced at resort ownership. They are investors who do not know that the ski industry is not easy. It cannot be run from a desk; it requires *on skis* type management. Joe and Joanne were *on skis* managers.

Before we leave the Weirick years, 1964–1978, we will take a quick look back and see what was accomplished.

During the Weirick Years:

9-15-1964
China Peak was purchased from Taylor-Wheeler Co.

1964
Rebuilt the old dorm, added the T-bar for beginners
Built the new parking area near the hotel
Added twelve new rooms to the hotel
Enlarged the Day Lodge

1966
Opened Chair #2

1968
Opened Fire Bowl T-Bar

1969
Had record snows, 30' deep at Day Lodge

1973
Opened Chair #3

1975
Built the new parking area near the hotel

1976
Added the first snow-making unit

1977
5000 people attend "China Sun" concert

1978
Sold China Peak to Bagdasarian-Harris Co.

CHAPTER 6

The Bagdasarian-Harris Era

On February 2, 1978, the *Fresno Bee*, by Omer Crane:

Fresnans Purchase China Peak

The long-rumored sale of the China Peak ski resort at Huntington Lake has been confirmed by the new owners, Fresno attorneys Gary G. Bagdasarian and Thomas W. Harris, Jr. "We expect to close escrow before Feb. 15," said Harris.

The purchase price is an even $4 million. Harris and his 28 year old partner, Bagdasarian, a Fresno native, who calls himself an intermediate skier, are putting up $1 million of their own and have borrowed $3 million from the Union Bank of Bavaria (West Germany). Harris said they are also negotiating to purchase Northstar, a resort on 2,500 acres of timberland owned by Trimont Co., a subsidiary of Fiberboard. The price tag on 100% of Trimont stock is $6.2 million, Harris added.

This statement by the *Fresno Bee* ushered in the next era in the never-ending drama that plays out in the history of our favorite ski resort. The Weiricks, Joe and Joanne, accepted the lawyers' offer and said goodbye to the faithful employees who had helped them for the last thirteen years. The trusted people who had worked so hard to keep this ski area running smooth through the drought years of 1975 to 1977 waved a "so-long" with more than one tear in the eye. The bar served drink after drink to be raised in toasts to the departing friends, and in salutes to the new owners. Champagne corks popped as Joe and Joanne drove out of the parking lot for the last time as the mom and pop owners of China Peak.

Many of the employees stayed on to work for the new owners, but some chose to move on. Harris and Bagdasarian named a new manager, John Crofut, to run the day-to-day operations at China Peak. The resort enjoyed great snows for the winter of 1978, but soon trouble was simmering in the Fresno offices. The statements given to reporter Omer Crane and reported in the *Fresno Bee* were most interesting.

I had found the article as part of my research for this book; and as I read and re-read it many times, I was intrigued by these two young attorneys. I found it interesting that these men, who knew nothing about the ski resort business, and by their own admissions were not even avid skiers, would purchase China Peak. I was curious as to how they met, how they became wealthy enough to put together a $4 million deal and then, even before escrow closed on China Peak, went shopping for another resort. They had also announced to the public their intentions to buy Northstar, near Lake Tahoe, with a price tag of $6.2 million.

I interviewed Mr. Bagdasarian at his office on June 11, 2008, and found him to be very helpful in explaining the strange chapter of their ownership. This is the story as he related it to me that day.

Gary G. Bagdasarian and Thomas W. Harris, Jr. had formed a two-man law partnership shortly after Bagdasarian returned to Fresno from obtaining his law degree. He had met Harris earlier while working as a law clerk for another firm. Harris was involved in doing tax work for his clients, and in that capacity often helped them find investments. One of his clients was Dorothy Schwartz, the widow of wealthy Fresno County rancher, Charley Schwartz.

Charley died April 7, 1976 of a heart attack at his ranch near Strathmore, California. Dorothy had lived in the mountains, and wanted a "mountain type investment," as she put it.

The two young lawyers set up a limited liability partnership, naming themselves, Gary G. Bagdasarian and Thomas W. Harris, Jr., as general partners, and Dorothy Schwartz as the limited partner. Dorothy had put up $4 million of her own money to purchase China Peak.

I asked Bagdasarian to clarify the statement that the *Fresno Bee* printed, stating that he and Harris were putting up $1 million of their own money, and they were borrowing $3 million from The Bank of Bavaria.

"It was all her money," was Bagdasarian's reply.

Fewer than six months after the purchase, Dorothy was unhappy with the arrangement, and wanted to end the partnership. "I want my money out; I want to invest it in another investment," Dorothy told her partners. She did not want to wait for the resort to be put on the market and sold. She was upset, and went to her own counsel, Jack Baker, a prominent Fresno lawyer.

A demand was made for the return of her money. The court transferred all the assets of the limited partnership to a receivership, and named attorney Richard Ford the receiver. Ford was not related to Schwartz, but was merely the person appointed by the court to protect the assets of the partnership. His job was to oversee the operation of the ski area and to protect Dorothy's investment. The partnership of Bagdasarian, Harris, and Schwartz was eventually dissolved.

I interviewed attorney Jack Baker by telephone on June 18, 2008. He explained to me that Dorothy wanted out of the partnership and wanted her money back. Mr. Baker filed a motion on her behalf and the case eventually went to trial.

In the subsequent trial, Mr. Baker requested the return of all of Dorothy Schwartz's investment. She and her partners had also invested in a hotel in Hawaii. The two attorneys, Bagdasarian and Harris, had claimed ownership of China Peak, but the court found in favor of Schwartz, and ordered ownership of the ski resort and the hotel in Hawaii returned to her. This provided a clear ownership of China Peak to Dorothy Schwartz Rojas (she had remarried), and she had a buyer in mind.

The name, China Peak, would soon melt like the snow in springtime, to trickle down the mountain streams, washed clean by pebbles and boulders alike, and soon dissolve into California lakes. It becomes just a memory to the old-time skiers who have skied the runs and enjoyed chili and beer on the sundeck. We have skied every run, every trail, both difficult and smooth, on sunny days and stormy days. A new name will be coming soon; the new owners are hoping to erase some bad karma left behind.

CHAPTER 7

New Owners, New Name

Each new season, when skiers come out for their first day, they are looking for new changes, better facilities and smoother runs. Nothing had changed for the last few years.

When news that the resort had been sold, it was met with guarded optimism. We, the employees, and the skiing public, had been let down before, and did not know what to expect from our new owners. Rumors had drifted around like fat snowflakes and piled up on top of one another, adding to the anxiety level. It was rumored that the resort had been sold to Japanese investors. Another rumor had it that the resort was closing, and all the lifts would be dismantled. None of the rumors were correct, which is often the case with gossip. When the true story was finally made public, it was welcome news, to be sure.

After three years of drifting like a rudderless ship, China Peak was ready to take up a new heading. The strides and improvements attributed to the Weiricks had not been followed with anything new. The paint was peeling and maintenance had been neglected. The attorneys were finished arguing in courtrooms and ownership had finally been established.

China Peak was purchased by Snow Summit Ski Corporation from Dorothy Schwartz Rojas. Escrow closed in December, 1981. It was decided to not change the name immediately. The resort was in such a sad state, the new owners were not quite ready to change its identity yet. That would come in due time. When it came, the name change was intended to send the signal that a new era was beginning, and put an end to an older period that was less than successful.

SNOW SUMMIT

Snow Summit was one of the first ski resorts in southern California, located near Big Bear Lake. It is the original resort owned by the Snow Summit Ski Corporation. It was started by Tommi Tyndall in the 1940s, and has grown to be one of the most successful ski areas in California. In spite of the fact that it is located in a very dry section of the state, and is relative small in size, Snow Summit has ranked in the top twenty of over 500 ski resorts in the nation in business volume. Snow Summit has been characterized throughout its more than fifty year history by a management that has always striven to offer a quality experience from the perspective of its customers.

During the early years of operation, Snow Summit had many winters when Mother Nature provided little or no natural snow. The winter of 1960–1961 provided only enough snow for fourteen days of operation. That was the year when a pivotal decision was made by Tommi Tyndall and his board of directors—to install snowmaking equipment. The cost was $300,000, and it was a huge investment at the time, but one that would spell the difference between failure and success.

Tommi was killed in a tragic tractor accident while maintaining a ski run in 1964. The baton was then passed to his wife, Jo, with her son Dick Kun as her assistant. Dick was named the general manager in 1972, when Jo was elected president. Dick has guided its growth and success ever since, and his years of experience have benefited Sierra Summit greatly. He has literally grown up in the ski resort business, and has guided Snow Summit through the good years and the not-so-good years. Dick is an expert skier, a certified ski instructor, and definitely a hands-on manager. He had skied at China Peak before, and knew what he and his corporation were buying.

THE END OF CHINA PEAK

The Snow Summit Ski Corporation has a long history of successfully running a ski resort, and was ready for a new challenge. China Peak was going fulfill that need and much more. Dick turned to his trusted mountain manager, Fred Goldsmith, to run their new resort. Fred, however, was happy where he was, and respectfully declined the offer.

Pete Scarparo was in the office at the time, and Dick turned to him and said, "How about you Pete? Do you want the job?"

Pete jumped at the opportunity to manage his own resort. He had been with Snow Summit since 1979, starting as a security officer. He was initially working as a security officer with another firm that was hired to patrol Snow Summit.

Dick is president of the Snow Summit Ski Corporation, the owners of Sierra Summit and its sister-resorts Snow Summit and Bear Mountain. He is also an excellent skier and a certified instructor.

Pete was instructed to keep everyone off the slopes before the resort opened, when he noticed a tall slender skier on cross-country skis, traversing the area. He intercepted the gate-crasher and did not believe a word the guy said when he told Pete he ran the resort. It was Dick Kun, the general manager of Snow Summit, on his way to work! That chance meeting led to an association that lasted many years. Pete was hired as a security guard, and his first job was managing the parking area. He moved up the ladder quickly, and when the resort needed a dozer operator, Pete was picked.

Pete quickly demonstrated a superb ability to get things done. Whatever needed to be fixed or built, Pete knew what do. Dick certainly picked the right guy to do this difficult job. With Pete Scaparo as the new General Manager and Dick Kun as head of the corporation, changes were in the works. The snowmaking experience of Snow Summit would prove invaluable to Sierra Summit.

Pete arrived at his new post in the fall of 1981, and escrow closed on December 21 of that year. He was handed the keys by Richard Ford, the attorney who was appointed to oversee operations while the resort spent five years in receivership. The ownership questions had finally been resolved. Pete was not impressed with the conditions that he found. The resort had no open charge accounts with their suppliers, and all business was cash on delivery. Credit and accounts had to be established and they took sixty to ninety days to open. In the meantime, Pete used Snow Summit's accounts and credit cards to get the business going.

Pete's new manager's residence had been used as a dog house, and it took considerable cleaning just to be made livable. Pete's wife, Maureen, and his two daughters, Kim and Jennifer, waited until the following spring to move to the resort. The name China Peak would not be changed to Sierra Summit until the beginning of the second season.

From left to right: Kim, Jennifer, Maureen and Pete Scaparo. Pete was general manager of Sierra Summit from 1981 until 2001, and Maureen was his Administration Assistant. The family lived at the resort in the manager's residence just behind the Sierra Summit Inn. The girls attended local schools and literally grew up at the resort. *Photo courtesy the Scaparo collection.*

Very little maintenance had been done in the last several years. Things got repaired when they absolutely had to be fixed to operate; otherwise, work was postponed. Pete inherited many problems. A less capable manager would have turned right around and gone back to southern California. Challenges were not new to Pete; he was used to working long hard hours, and not being satisfied until the job was done. In December, Pete hired Pat "Boomer" Devaurs and Bob "Otto" Horen to cut trees and burn brush. Both would turn out to be long time employees. Boomer is now marketing director.

The year of 1981 was not a good year for the financial world or the ski world. It was a challenging time to own a ski resort; still, Sierra Summit had a good year, with 134,000 skier visits.

John Fry in *Skiing Heritage,* June 2008.

The stock market plunged 27 percent. The ski market unhappily fell, too. Lack of snow caused skier visits to fall by 19% to below 40 million. Indeed, the winter of 1980–1981 generated only 39.7 million skier-days, the lowest ever recorded by the National Ski Areas Association since it began record-keeping in 1978–1979. Colorado resorts were especially hard hit. Breckenridge's skier-visits fell from 724,000 to 195,000.

Sierra Summit survived that first year, proving that they were in the game to stay!

SUMMER, 1982

In the summer of 1982, the name was officially changed to Sierra Summit, Inc., D.B.A. Sierra Summit Ski Resort. A new

Here is Pete Scaparo, the general manager from 1981 until 2001, clearing new runs on the West Ridge. Pete was equally at home behind his desk and operating the company D-6 cat. He was talented in both duties, and cherished his summers doing big jobs improving the runs. *Photo courtesy Pete Scaparo collection.*

During the construction of the new Chair #1, many trees were removed from the runs. They were lifted up by a heavy lift helicopter and carried down to waiting trucks. The helicopter then picked up the new towers, flew them up to their positions and placed them on their foundations. *Photo courtesy Pete Scaparo collection.*

Long Range Development Plan was being developed to be submitted to the U.S.F.S. for approval. The Snow Summit Ski Corporation had decided to invest $1.4 million in improvements in the new resort.

The decision was made to start on the following major upgrades:

1. Split Chair #2 into two separate lifts. The top half would remain Chair #2, and serve upper intermediate and expert runs. The bottom half would become Chair #4, and serve the lower runs, Lower Tollhouse, and Academy. Chair #4 would be converted to a triple chair. This conversion would make two short, high capacity lifts out of one older long, low capacity lift, plus putting an unloading ramp for Chair #4 and a loading station for Chair #2 midway up the mountain.

2. A new loading area was built at the base of Chair #4.

3. Improve Midway Foods and add a temporary 20' × 40' restroom facility.

4. Start clearing all runs of stumps, rocks, and dead trees. Two new runs were opened: Ridge Run and Sundown Ridge.

5. Remodel the hotel and rework the food service and bar. The Day Lodge was remodeled, and updated.

6. The old locker room near the pool was remodeled to become the new business office.

7. The kitchen had to be torn apart to remove two old diesel-fired boilers in the heating plant. One thing seemed to lead to another, and in the end, much of the plumbing, heating, and electrical was replaced. The old boilers were replaced with propane-fired units that were much cleaner burning. These could be used singly or in tandem on colder days.

8. Add new equipment: a new diesel-powered snow-blower, a new Caterpillar 966 Loader, and a used D-6 Caterpillar dozer. Several Snowcats from the Snow Summit fleet were trucked in to help. It takes a mighty fleet of equipment to keep the runs groomed and the parking lots cleared. This was just the start; much more would be added later.

9. The existing sewer plant needed to be upgraded. It was rebuilt, adding a cathodic unit for corrosion protection. This is a modern plant designed by civil engineer Dennis Keller. The plant is capable of handling 10,000 people per day. All material is digested by anaerobic bacteria, and all effluent is tested daily to assure quality.

10. The first brochure with the name *Sierra Summit* was printed for the start of the '82–'83 season.

11. The new diesel truck, known ever after as the "Town Truck," was added to the fleet. This is the Freightliner with the 40' trailer, both beautifully painted with the Sierra Summit logo on the sides that is often seen on

Highway 168. This truck and trailer rig makes an almost daily trip to Fresno to pick up needed parts and supplies for the resort. In addition to this trailer is a flatbed trailer that is used to move snowcats and grooming equipment to and from the sister resorts, wherever they are needed. The trailer also has side rails to haul logs to the sawmill, which is an additional source of revenue for the resort.

The improvements made during the summer and the increased radio and media advertising efforts really paid off. The first season's skier count of 134,000 was increased by 28% to a new record of 171,000, and 29,000 ahead of the old China Peak record of 142,000, set in 1979.

The winter of 1982–1983 was one of the best snow years, much better than the previous winters. The resort opened early on November 11th, and ended late on April 20th. There were so many snow storms, especially on weekends, that

More deep powder in January of 2008— and just think, this was not the best of years. Keep your skis ready, so when a storm hits you can sneak in some hot powder runs.

the heavy snows actually kept many skiers away. Before the Christmas holiday, during the very busiest part of the season, the area was hit with 100 mph winds, uprooting many ice-laden trees, causing extensive damage to Chairs #2 and #3. When Pete and his crew assessed the damage, it was obvious that many of the cross-arms and chairs would have to be replaced, and the cable would need to be inspected for damage. The parts were ordered from the Riblet factory in Spokane, Washington and the factory began fabricating the new parts the following day. The new Town Truck was dispatched to pick up the needed parts. By the time it arrived at the factory, the parts were finished. The truck was loaded and turned around for the return trip. There was no time to waste. This is the busy season, and closed lifts mean lost business. (Brian Bressel, who would later become general manager, was the driver.)

Crews were sent in from Snow Summit to start dismantling the damaged parts. When the truck returned from Washington, the crews began installing the new cross-arms. The lifts were back in full operation in less than a week. This is just normal procedure for the Sierra Summit family! The first year under the Sierra Summit banner, the resort set a new record in skier visits, and one that would be hard to match in future years.

Extensive snowmaking equipment was planned for Sierra Summit, but this wonderful season made it easy to think that this was the norm and not the exception. Maybe the huge expense of installing permanent snowmaking equipment like that Snow Summit had would be unnecessary after all. Snow Summit is located in a very dry area of California, and regular natural snowfall was never taken for granted. Sierra Summit is in an area with great natural snow, or so it seems. This line of thought would soon prove to be wrong. Mother Nature can never be depended upon in California. If you want dependable snow year after year, you have to be ready to make it yourself.

SUMMER, 1983

Much more extensive remodeling work was accomplished on the east wing of the hotel. It was converted from employee housing to much needed hotel rooms. Twenty new double-wide mobile homes were purchased for employee housing; ten were three-bedrooms, and ten were two-bedrooms. One unit was placed near the hotel, where it would become the general manager's residence, and the others were placed in an area behind the back parking lots. One unit was to be used as the company store, a TV room, and a laundry room, with washers and dryers for the employees. Remember, employees here do not have access to the city conveniences and many are housed on company property. Some meals and lodging are furnished. In addition, each mobile home had a shared kitchen for those who wanted to prepare their own meals.

This company store serves the needs of the employees who live at the resort through the winter season. It's not a big-box shopping center, but it stocks the little necessities of life. Many of the residents are workers from South America, Australia, New Zealand, as well as other countries, and don't have cars or access to town. *Photo courtesy Sierra Summit.*

The hotel and restaurant were opened for summer tourists, and the chairlift was operated for sight-seeing trips.

SKI SEASON, 1983–1984

The ski season was plagued by clear weather, with snowfall well below normal. The resort operated 117 days and had 129,000 skier days, well below the hoped-for totals. Because of the superior run preparation done by Pete and his crew the summer before, we were able to ski on very thin snow. Plans were prepared for many improvements to make Sierra Summit more attractive not only to the local skier, but to attract more skiers from outside the Fresno area as well.

SUMMER, 1984

Another summer and another million dollars were invested to increase capacity. Chair #5, a 3000-foot lift to near

The blue of the crystal clear sky blends with the fresh snow bank on this beautiful day in March 2006. This was taken from near the unloading ramp of Chair #2 looking toward Chair #5. Blue sky and fresh snow combine to make the day perfect.

This is the run that the locals head to after a storm. It is steep; it is expert terrain and it is no place for the weak of heart. But, oh what a rewarding blast it is for the expert skier.

What a great view from the top of China Bowl looking down the top of Kaiser and the unloading ramp of Chair #2. Days like this are to die for, to be cherished in the mind of the hard-core skier. Well worth calling in sick, just hope your boss is not on the same run!

the top of Chinese Peak, the highest point on the ski area, was completed, adding 150 feet to the overall vertical drop. It opens up Chinese Bowl to advanced and high intermediate skiers. The new triple-seat Chair #5 runs from Midway to the top of the mountain, and it serves all runs from the peak. This beautiful bowl was sure to be a great hit. We hearty souls had hiked up to ski it for years, and now it was going public. A major new advanced run, Dynamite, was built on the east side of Chair #3. The new runs and quality improvements were aimed at making the Central California skier market more competitive with Mammoth and the Tahoe Ski Areas.

The Day Lodge underwent a much needed clean-up and improvement, including new paint. The new garbage compaction station was installed at the back parking lot #1, as work was started on a new food facility at Midway. It was to be named Midway Day Lodge. As an old saying goes, "the best laid plans." Yes, the best laid plans sometimes never get completed. Midway Day Lodge, a 7000 square foot facility, was never built. The picnic and eating area was finally added, but it is nowhere as grand as the big new Day Lodge that exists only in artists' drawings. All that was built originally were the footings, which are still visible, just north of the picnic area. We still only had one men's and one women's restroom at Midway. Blame the poor snow year that just passed; maybe the next year would be better. But, in California, there is no such thing as a "normal snow year." There are years that are above average in snowfall, and years that are below average, but we don't know what normal is. We hoped next year would be better.

There was much construction going on in the Huntington Lake area during this time. To be more specific, much construction was going on underground, expanding the Big Creek Tunnels to the electric power generating plant. Soil from this excavation, known as tunnel muck, was trucked to Sierra Summit from an excavation site near Huntington. This was used to form the base for two new parking lots. It provided the fill material to level the surface, and would later be covered with asphalt. Six trucks, running daily for three

This was the ski-up window in the early Midway. There were
outdoor picnic tables, and restrooms in the rear of the building.
The shelter for the picnic tables and the indoor food preparation
area were added later.

A Bombardier 2000 snow grooming machine cuts through heavy new powder
on this early morning first run on February 21, 2005. The new shelter at
Midway keeps the picnic tables and the picnickers snug and dry. This is a great
place to stop for hot chocolate on a great morning such as this.

weeks, hauled enough material to cover the parking lots with material one foot deep. The trucks completed the eight mile round trip, traveling four miles on the highway, and four miles off-road.

SKI SEASON, 1984–1985

The following season of 1984–1985 was another "less than average" snow year, with some runs not having adequate coverage until mid-March. Even with this rather poor start for the year, Sierra Summit enjoyed a banner year for skiers. Without any doubt, the new Chair #5 made all the difference in the world. It quickly became the favorite of the top echelon of expert skiers. Sierra Summit had one of their best years ever, ending the ski-season with a near record skier-day count

One picture is sometimes worth many words. After a long day of skiing, getting out of the parking lot could be a problem. The parking lots were regraded and leveled with tunnel-muck trucked in from tunnel work near Huntington Lake. They were paved not long after this picture was taken. The lots are plowed after storms, and are now easy to enter and leave. *Photo courtesy Pete Scaparo collection.*

of 165,000 visits, and well above the previous year count of 129,000. Management had tightened their proverbial belts to the last notch, and squeaked out a tidy profit, much to the delight of the new owners. Their heavy investing in improvements pleased even the pickiest of skiers and customers, and they were proving to be wise decisions. The late arrival of winter and the delayed opening of some runs, pointed more and more to the need for higher capacity snowmaking. It was becoming ever more obvious that a successful resort could not depend on California's stingy snow-gods to guarantee on time delivery of perfect white snow every winter, all winter.

SUMMER, 1985

The new Midway Day Lodge was put on indefinite hold. Maybe it would be completed the next summer and then, maybe not. There were other, more important upgrades that could be done with less capital outlay. The widening and cleaning up of all ski runs and the re-grooming of China Bowl took precedence. This work continued all summer, with General Manager Pete Scaparo doubling as the dozer operator. He was equally at home at his desk or running the dozer.

The huge new propane storage tank was installed in the base area, at the back of parking lot #1. A three-inch gas main was installed to all base area buildings: the hotel, the Day Lodge, employee housing, and all boilers. All of the old 1000 gallon tanks were removed from individual buildings. This resulted in larger bulk deliveries at lower cost.

SKI SEASON, 1985–1986

Sierra Summit had its third straight year of below normal snowfall, as did all of the Sierra resorts, which experienced the same mild and wet season that brought quite a bit of rain below the 8000 foot level. Sierra Summit was not the only one that was short of snow. All the other California resorts

This cute little snack bar was mounted on skids, and could be positioned just about anyplace. Here it is shown in the base area; the new Mainline Station put this little shack into early retirement. *Photo courtesy Sierra Summit.*

were down, too. There would be continued development, but at a rather slower pace than previously anticipated.

SUMMER, 1986

The Snow Summit Ski Corporation had operated Sierra Summit for five years. It had invested millions in improvements; yet financial success was elusive. It was felt that by clearing runs and making them smoother, they would be skiable with lighter snow coverage, and natural snowfall would be adequate. After the third straight year of below normal snowfall, it was time to install a permanent snowmaking system. The first half of a rudimentary system was installed at a cost of $175,000. This was designed for spot coverage of certain high traffic areas that become exposed during periods of low snowfall. This system covered approximately the east half of the mountain from top to bottom. More capacity would be added later.

A slant-well was drilled to add to the capacity of two other wells nearby.

The pipeline was run from the 66,000 gallon storage tank in Fire Bowl to the top of Chairs #3, #1, #5, and #2. Water was pumped to the top of the mountains for snowmaking, and a separate buried pipe then gravity fed water down to Midway for domestic supply. Snow could be made from Midway down Express to the Last Face.

This upper system was used only two years, and the lower system used only one year before it was modified. Most pipelines in the Sierra Summit system are above ground, due to the rocky granite surface of the mountain. The system had to be run continuously or drained completely to prevent freezing.

SKI SEASON, 1986–1987

The ski industry as a whole was in a period of stagnant growth for many reasons. The increased cost of skiing for the

Here we see the powerful snow guns blasting out the white stuff. These guns are connected by hoses to two permanent pipes, one with compressed air, and the other water under high pressure. This mixture is mixed at the nozzle and sprayed into sub-freezing air, forming snow instantly.

public, and competition from other hobbies and pastimes were causing fewer new skiers to enter the market. Skiers were also becoming more sophisticated in their choice of places to ski. If the snow wasn't good at Sierra Summit, the Tahoe region might beckon for better skiing. The larger ski areas were installing more and more snowmaking equipment. Sierra Summit would have to do better snowmaking if it wanted to be competitive.

Sierra Summit's 1986–1987 ski season was the most disappointing of the six seasons that the Snow Summit Ski Corporation had operated it. It was far and away the worst year for natural snow since 1977. There were start and stop marginal operations earlier, but it was not until mid-February that the resort could run on a sustained basis. The season ended with a disappointing 69,000 skier-visits. Mammoth had conditions that were no better. Both Sierra Summit and Mammoth had a 50% loss off the average volume of recent years.

Employee morale hit a new low as well. There were two large mid-season layoffs. Some employees went to Snow Summit to work, which was faring a bit better due to its superior snowmaking system.

SUMMER, 1987

Ambitious plans were in the works for Sierra Summit. Snowmaking had always been planned to supplement natural snow, but now it was time to speed up the timetable. The Board of Directors made the decision to invest $550,000 in more improvements to protect their interests. It was obvious that more efficient snowmaking was needed if the resort was to survive. Without a doubt, the poor snowfall seasons confirmed the need for enhanced snowmaking abilities.

Pete Scaparo and Jim Laramore traveled to Whiteface Mountain Resort in New York to look at their system, which was also an above-ground installation. The rudimentary system was already in place, and more work would need to be done. A system was installed on the lower half of the mountain that would cover the high-traffic sections of runs where it was difficult to hold snow.

Hundreds of feet of used pipe were bought from the oil fields and experienced welders were hired to put the pipelines in place. After long summer months of working on the steep mountain sides, the job was completed. The pipeline was laid from the Midway section of the mountain down to the base area, completing the loop, and providing snowmaking for the lower portion of the runs. This would eventually be expanded and cover most of the area, but for now it would cover the lower half of the mountain. This was another step in what would become a very complex system. For the first years, it would cover some of the spots that get the heaviest skier use. The water for this system would be pumped at about 1200 gallons per minute through a closed system that kept the water circulating.

New snow for Christmas in December 2007 covers the lodge, the bridge and the frozen Big Creek. A welcome gift and just in time for the Holidays! The picture was taken just after boarding Chair #6, looking back.

The entire Beginner Area was re-graded and actually relocated to provide a ski hill close to the sundeck at the Day Lodge. This was a huge earth-moving project, changing the slope of the hill to a more west to east direction. A small rope tow and a T-bar lift were removed from the Bunny Hill and replaced with two handle tows running parallel to the Day Lodge. Before this change was made, all slopes descended toward the Day Lodge.

The Forest Service allowed the resort to use water from Big Creek for snowmaking purposes. The water is turned into snow, which remains on the mountain until spring. Some of the melted snow soaks into the ground, while some of it evaporates, but most of it melts and returns to the creek as water. For this reason, not much water is lost to the area; it is just borrowed, and then returned. Creek water had also been used for drinking and domestic water at the hotel and lodge, but that would no longer be allowed. New wells had to be drilled for drinking water. The wells feed into Fire Bowl tank, where a four-inch main delivered water to Midway and finally down to the holding tank near the hotel. Another new well near the hotel completed the system, providing adequate water for the hotel and lodges. Sierra Summit has a sophisticated water treatment plant and trained operators to insure guests of safe drinking water.

It is also interesting to note that a two-inch water line was placed under Highway 168 to furnish water to Gold Arrow Camp on the lake. This is one more example of Sierra Summit's commitment to be a good neighbor to the community. Water is often scarce in the mountains, and the resort is fortunate to have a good supply.

SKI SEASON, 1987–1988

The Sierra once again experienced a below normal snowfall, causing water shortages throughout the state. Sierra Summit had another terrible season of natural snowfall, similar to the previous season. The big difference this season was that the new snowmaking system on the lower half of the hill was in full operation. That new system, along with more aggressive marketing, accounted for a skier volume increase over the last year's season from 70,000 to 110,000.

SUMMER, 1988

Due to the proven success of snowmaking, a decision was made to invest another $450,000 to provide supplemental coverage for most major runs on the upper half of the mountain, including an additional 23,000 feet of pipeline, a second pump station, and a three million gallon reservoir. All five chairlifts, most major runs, and the beginner hill would now be operational for most of the ski season, even in dry winters, such as 1987 and 1988. All lifts had at least one run that was covered with snowmaking.

The Midway snowmaking pond was constructed just north of Academy, and the Midway snowmaking pump

Water is pumped up to this man-made pond from Big Creek, stored here until needed, and then turned into snow by the snow making system. Skiers whiz past this beautiful scene on Academy. What a great spot for a wine and cheese break on a sunny day.

house was built. The Edison Company ran power from the base area to operate the pumps. A covered water main was added, increasing the pumping capacity to 2000 gpm, up from 1200 gpm.

SKI SEASON, 1988–1989

The six-year drought continued in the Sierra. This season was the worst of the last three for natural snowfall. Fortunately, the completion of the snowmaking system on the upper half of the mountain enabled an increase of skier days to 132,000, up from the previous season total of 110,000. This was proving once again the value of snowmaking to a ski resort. The new system worked very well, and provided protection against poor natural snowfall. Snow could be made on most major runs, and the area capacity operated at nearly 100%, even with minimum natural snowfall.

SUMMER, 1989

The importance of making snow to supplement Mother Nature's winter work was now well established. Central California can experience weather swings from the deluges of wet years to the driest of dry years. The season's first snow storms can come as early as October or as late as January or February. With the proper snowmaking equipment in place, snow could be made anytime the temperatures remained below freezing. The optimum design would have permanent pipelines anchored in place on the mountain runs. The system requires a pipe to carry water under high pressure, and another to carry compressed air. There are hydrants at strategic points to attach hoses. Two hoses, one for compressed air, the other for water, are attached to guns pointed in the desired direction. The two ingredients are fed into the gun under pressure and mixed at the nozzle. The air-water mix exits the nozzle into the sub-freezing atmosphere and falls as snow. By 1989, the system was mostly completed, and all the bugs had been worked out; snowmaking was covering most of the major runs.

The basic snowmaking system was now in place. Specific areas of the mountain could be selected to provide higher concentration of snow where needed. The system was completed in time for the opening day of the 1989–1990 ski season.

SKI SEASON, 1989–1990

Unfortunately, the drought continued throughout the early winter months of the ski season. There was even less natural snow than the prior year, and only a few runs were operational on man-made snow until mid-January. The resort saw skier visits decline for the season, from 132,000 to 100,000. The company did make a small profit for the season, proving to themselves that the snowmaking investment was a success.

The ski season would have resulted in a profit, but an employee's mistake proved to be very costly. In the early spring of 1990, an expensive blunder resulted in the release of 2000 gallons of diesel fuel on the ground and into Big Creek. An employee was pumping fuel to fill a compressor in the equipment lot. When he finished, he did not shut the nozzle completely off, allowing the fuel to continue running through the night. This proved to be a very, very, expensive mistake. The Forest Service responded, along with no less than six other agencies, including the U.S. Coast Guard, as Big Creek water eventually enters the Pacific Ocean. Work was started immediately by diverting the creek to flow around the spill area. Temporary mitigation was started, and it continued all summer.

SUMMER, 1990

As soon as weather permitted, and as the snow melted, work began in earnest, cleaning up the creek. Eight hundred square yards of soil was removed from the creek banks, and spread out on plastic sheets in the back #1 parking lot. Bioremediation was started to encourage bacteria to clean the soil. Warm water was sprayed on the soil to hasten the bacterial process. All rocks and stones in the creek were scrubbed clean. By the end of the summer of 1990, the soil was ready to be reused.

Valuable lessons were learned. All of the old single-wall fuel storage tanks were removed and replaced with double-walled tanks. Five other slightly soiled areas were also cleaned up. In the end, the Forest Service commended the Sierra Summit Mountain Resort for a job well done. This was the first oil spill contamination at this altitude, and would serve as a model for years to come. This mistake cost $750,000, and it took years to recover the loss.

SKI SEASON, 1990–1991

Like other Sierra ski areas, Sierra Summit was again the victim of the California drought. This was the fifth straight year of well below normal snowfall. Not only would this drought hurt skiers for the year, but it looked as if many just might get out of the habit of skiing. If it had not been for the resort's expert snowmaking skills and careful grooming, they would not have had the moderate success they did. Natural snowfall did not cover the slopes until March. By that time, many skiers had lost the urge to ski. The economy was in a slump and many experts felt that skiers were turning to other leisure-time pursuits. Maybe they would forget how to ski, or just hang up the old planks and turn to a different sport. The Central California farm economy was also depressed and the Fresno market felt the repercussions. The season had less than 200 inches of snow—well below the average.

The ski industry is very closely related to the farming industry when it comes to dependence on the weather. It plays a huge factor in making the difference between failure versus profitability. Many other factors enter into the equation, such as marketing, economy, available demand, and total customer base. Most of these things are not controllable by the producer; in this case, the ski resort. However, managers can make some positive steps to control the outcome.

The motto of the successful ski resort manager might as well be, "make the best of what you have." Rather than dwell on the lack of deep snow in advertising, market the fact that plenty of sunshine graces our slopes. Pleasing the customer is vital to the success of any business, and keeping the skier happy in lean years as well as abundant snowfall years makes the difference between success and even better success. Skiers have become much more sophisticated in their choices of ski locations than ever before. The beautiful big ski resorts of the Tahoe area, as well as the expertly managed Mammoth, just on the other side of the Sierra, pose a constant temptation to the Fresno skier. The other California resorts are more tuned to the destination skier than Sierra Summit, offering other amenities such as shopping, gambling, fine dining, and entertainment.

The Sierra Summit management decided to start a market rebuilding process, with lower pricing, more school programs and youth programs. It was time for more belt-tightening: no more money would be spent on improvements or new equipment until the skier market improved.

Now might be the time to take a good look back at history and make a comparison. The cost of a room in the hotel in 1960 was $8.00, and a lift ticket was $5.00. The prices for the present season, 2007–2008 are: hotel room, $60.00, and lift ticket, $46.00. Inflation accounts for much of the increase, but the added costs of snowmaking, improved water quality, and high liability insurance rates all must be taken into consideration as well. Still, compared to the other resorts in California, these prices are a bargain.

In the late 1980s, a change was in the air. The Snow Summit Ski Corporation had invested millions of dollars into making Sierra Summit into a well-run quality resort, and the returns on their investments were unspectacular, to say the least. Pete Scaparo and an investor were interested in buying the resort. They put together a package of their plans for the future, but in the end they could not raise the needed capital to close the sale, and the deal fell apart.

SUMMER, 1991

Undaunted by a poor ski year just passed, work continued throughout the summer. The full-time employees had to be kept busy; without fulltime jobs, they wouldn't stay.

A recycling center was built on the back lot, #1, next to the garbage compacting system. The area was now recycling everything usable. Instead of the truck making two trips a week to the dump, Sierra Summit was actually selling recycled material. Fresno County was so impressed that they gave an award to Sierra Summit's recycling program.

SKI SEASON, 1991–1992

Sierra Summit operated on man-made snow through December. Then the snow-gods finally started to smile, if only just a little bit. The season started a bit slow, but due to great snowmaking, December proved to be a good month, and even better snows came in January. The California Ski industry was in a distressing slump, caused by the lingering drought and the economic recession caused by the Gulf War, but some skiers, and more and more snowboarders, were starting to return. The new lower prices for mid-week skiing proved very popular, indeed. Sierra Summit hosted 127,000 skiers for the season, and the company reported a tidy profit of over $100,000.

SUMMER, 1992

Extensive run clearing—removing brush, stumps, and rocks—is the never-ending task of improving slopes to make them better for skiing with less snow. The runs that needed three feet of snow just a few years ago now became very ski-able with twelve to twenty-four inches of snow.

SKI-SEASON, 1992–1993

Skiers have often joked that in order to please the snow-gods, they would do whatever it takes, including sacrificing virgins. They were just kidding of course (at least I think they were kidding). Whatever they did, it worked in the winter of 1992. The snow just fell, and fell, and continued falling! The season started early and lasted late, giving the snowmaking crew a needed rest. Snow only had to be made in some high traffic areas, cutting down on snowmaking costs. The season ended with a record snowfall of over 400 inches, and visits of 151,000 happy skiers and boarders. For the first five years of Snow Summit's ownership, the area averaged 145,000 skier days. During the worst of the drought years, the average had fallen to only 100,000.

SUMMER, 1993

The wonderful ski season just past re-sparked the owners' interest in continued growth. The midweek pricing brought out new skiers and boarders, and the resort was profitable again. Possibly, happy days were here again! The hotel was open for full operation, for the first summer operation since 1988. It was a money loser that year, but maybe this year would be better. The booming new sport of mountain bicycling was off to a modest start. Sunday, June 20th, was the Reg Bauer-sponsored China Peak Classic mountain bike race, from the Day Lodge up the mountain to the "Chinaman's Cabin," and back. This was the cabin of the Chinese boy that was adopted to cook for the Blasingame family (the same boy that was mentioned early in my history of China Peak), and the cabin is still standing.

SKI SEASON, 1993–1994

Gol dang it, what happened to the snow? We thought the drought was over, but we did not have any natural snow this winter until mid-January. The snowmaking equipment once again saved the season. Very little natural snow fell until February, but the base was in place, and with snowmaking, the season finished with a profit to the company. Skier visits were down to 127,000 from the previous season of 151,000.

The Central California and Fresno skier base continued to grow, and with strong marketing and advertising, Sierra Summit was gaining skiers through the important midweek days. Special pricing and aggressive school programs were adding skiers on otherwise quiet times. Students were offered a special Sunday rate of $10.00 to build the youth market.

SUMMER, 1994

More run clearing continued to improve the area. No big area projects were started this year, but plans were in the works if a good season came in the next year.

SKI SEASON, 1994–1995

Wow! Talk about great snow! The snow-gods had finally awakened to our prayers. We don't know what we did to deserve it, but we had the best snow since 1969. Over 450 inches of the greatest white stuff this side of Utah. Is this a return to the "normal snow pattern?" We hoped so. This season saw 161,000 skier days, the third highest volume since Sierra Summit emerged from China Peak. Sierra Summit rewarded its corporate owners with the highest profit since the '80s. There is nothing like a handsome profit to turn the management folks' line of thinking to improving the area. Several years had passed since serious investing had given us any major changes. That thinking was about to change; the switch was once again moved to the development mode.

Karen Powell shoveling snow at old Midway. This little old building that housed the food preparation is buried in about six feet of new powder in this April 2006 storm. More proof that our heaviest storms come late in the season. February, March and April offer great skiing, longer days and fewer crowds.

SUMMER, 1995

Changes were in store for Sierra Summit Skiers. The first major improvements since 1985 were coming, and they were directly related to the last year's profitability. Bottlenecks and traffic jams had hampered the base area forever and ever. Skiers would get suited up and walk out the door on the snow, only to be met by long lines of skiers at the lifts, waiting to get out of the base area onto the mountain. The backup of skiers all trying to leave the base area at the same time made the mountain look crowded, but when they exited the lift at the top and looked around, it looked empty. The problem had been inadequate lift capacity leaving the base area. It was a problem that had existed for the entire lifetime of Sierra Summit.

CHAPTER 8

Old Chairs, New Chairs

In what seemed like a counter-productive move, Chair #1 was abandoned, and the upper towers were removed. The lower towers, the terminal, and the lower bull-wheel were left in place, to be used again later. The plan at the time was to replace the old Chair #1 with a new lift the following year. The upper towers were stored for future use. Actually, not all the towers were stored; one was installed to support the Sierra Summit sign that you see as you turn off the highway and into the parking lot. The upper terminal that housed the drive unit and the bull-wheel were remodeled, a deck was added, and the structure was modified to become a Ski Patrol station.

A new Chair #1 was installed near Chair #3 to add to the lift capacity from the base area. This is a triple chair lift that was first used at Snow Summit, and was replaced after ten years by a high-speed quad. It was handed down, or handed up, as the case may be, to Sierra Summit. This is Sierra Summit's third triple chair, and would greatly speed up lift capacity on busy days. It is closer to the main parking areas, and it would require a shorter walk for skiers from car to ski lift. This "new to us" lift delivers skiers to almost the same place that old Chair #1 did from 1958 to 1995. The new bull wheel and unloading terminal are within sight of the old terminal of Chair #1. How many hundreds of times we have ridden old #1? One can only imagine.

Pete Scaparo and his D6 Dozer worked all summer clearing ten new runs, clearing brush, and felling trees. Helicopters

There is an interesting bit of history here. This is the structure that housed the motor-drive unit and the bull-wheel of the original Chair #1, which was built in 1958. It was closed permanently on June 1, 1991, never to run again. A new Chair #1 was built to replace this lift; the bull-wheel and motor-drive unit is now located about one hundred feet east.

Here a group of employees that made the last ride on the old lift pose for a photo and enjoy the late season snow for one last run. From left to right they are: Mark Reigle, Eric Winkler, Frank Bressel, Boomer Devaurs, Dawna Lord, Karen Dormier, Benita Lodge, Phil Kerridge, Brian Bressel, Steve Gillett and Bruce Gillett. After the bull-wheel was moved, the upper level was remodeled to become the first on-hill ski patrol station. The motor-drive unit still sits rusting in the lower level of the building. *Photo courtesy Rich Bailey collection.*

were used to carry out logs, loading them onto the truck to go to the sawmill. The helicopters would then deliver the towers to be mounted on their cement bases. The new lift, which is now named Chair #1 (just to confuse us), was ready for the first snow of the winter.

Some of the new runs were on the west side of the mountain and would be served in the future by a new chair. We have skied these areas for years, but had to wait for new powder to "ski the trees." With the runs now clear and smooth, we would be skiing on days when the snowpack was less.

Here in the front is Boomer Devaurs, Stevo Gillett, and Rich Bailey. In the rear are Pete Scaparo, Pat Macartea and Brian Bressel. The staff heads for a high level management meeting by way of Chair #1. *Photo courtesy Pete Scaparo collection.*

The hotel and restaurant stayed open for the summer. Mountain biking was growing in popularity and many of the winter skiers were summer bicyclists.

SKI SEASON, 1995–1996

There are good snow years, and poor snow years. The winter of 1995–1996 was a poor year—a below average snow year—and only delivered slightly over half of the snow of the previous year. Snowmaking, which had been improved every year since the initial installation, again saved the season. Without snowmaking, Sierra Summit would have been closed for most of the winter. As it was, Sierra Summit was only in partial operation, primarily on man-made snow, until mid January. Two more weeks of rain after that really screwed things up. Finally, heavy snowfall came, and it provided good skiing conditions until April. The many improvements that were made the previous summer were met with unbridled enthusiasm.

The local skiers were suitably impressed, and many new skiers came out to enjoy the new runs. The five new runs on the west side were scheduled to get their own chair the previous summer, but that improvement had to wait. The season ended with 123,000 skier visits, down 21% over the previous year.

SUMMER, 1996

In the summer of 1996, Sierra Summit once again offered mountain biking, using the new Chair #1 to carry riders to a network of trails and roads. The hotel and restaurant was again open during the summer, and the increased bike operations attracted new visitors. A new chair was to be installed that same summer, but due to financial and other constraints, it would also have to wait. This was the last year the hotel and restaurant would be open. The swimming pool had been filled in and cemented over back in 1990, and the happy days of swimming at Sierra Summit had come to an end.

SKI SEASON, 1996–1997

Sierra Summit had a more "normal" winter with adequate natural snow. The problem was that most of it fell, along with a great deal of rain, during the Christmas holidays and January, at the height of the season. To say that this dampened ski enthusiasm is an understatement. Many families plan holiday ski trips, and nothing causes kids to get cranky faster than snow mixed with rain. People pack up the car and head downhill fast when storms move in. The weather turned mild and dry from early February through the end of the season. There was plenty of snow by that time, but the lack of continuous snowfall discouraged many visitors. Skiers would prefer it to snow every week to provide clean white cover for our skiing pleasure, but this is asking too much. The season ended with 123,000 skier visits, down from the previous year, but still profitable.

SUMMER, 1997

As has happened during many summers before, and will happen for many summers in the future, not much construction takes place after a poor ski season. The constant maintenance continues, but there are no big improvement expenditures. The chairlift for the new runs on the west side slipped farther into the future. We had hoped for a better season the next winter. Skiers had always hoped for better winters, earlier snows, and more spring snow. Where was that normal winter? Where was that perfect winter when heavy snows occurred during the week, and the weekends dawned clear and white, with mountains frosted with new powder?

SKI SEASON, 1997–1998

The heavy snows finally arrived, courtesy of El Nino. Heavy snowfalls made for a spectacular season, and at

Always the most popular spot on the whole ski area, the sun deck is THE place to see and be seen. This is the place to watch the action on the entire lower half of the mountain. It is also interesting to note the deep snow, reaching almost to the level of the second-floor deck.

times, resulted in too much snow. Storms and winter road conditions discouraged many visitors. Everybody wants to ski on fresh white powder, but not many people want to ski during storms. Driving in the Sierra Mountains during storm conditions can be difficult, even hazardous. Radio and television stations broadcast constant winter storm warnings, and this certainly limits the number of visits, especially families. Kids don't like storms, and even though we now see kids outfitted with the best Gore-Tex clothing, it's just not as much fun.

Snowboarders are becoming a larger and larger part of the market. What began as a very small segment of the customer base, and one that was really not too welcome, was now becoming a very important piece of the resort business. Snowboarders were maturing, and becoming more easily accepted by skiers. We were now finding that more snowboarders have had lessons, and they are better able to control their speed and direction, resulting in fewer skier collisions. Snowboarders continued to be a "special breed," and therefore had different ideas of fun.

A skier relishes in speed, whistling wind, and the beauty of the mountains. The more mature snowboarders look for smooth runs, room to turn, and independence. Young boarders, on the other hand, like to be in the midst of the snowboard crowd, performing their own forms of tricks and fun. The season ended with the wonderful snowfall total of over 400 inches and a total skier visits of 156,000. The good news did not end there; the corporation reported record profits for the year!

SUMMER, 1998

Snowboarders yearn for an audience, with jumps, bumps, and rails to show off their skills and bravado. There are still the macho types, but more and more, they were becoming better citizens. They were here to stay, so why not make things better for them? Sierra Summit did just that. They built a special snowboard park. The first park was built in the summer of 1998. It was small by today's standards, but it was a start. It was going to be the first try at what would be a trial and error attempt to see what pleased the boarders. They love jumps, rails, and half-pipes, and Sierra Summit has something to please everyone. It is to our benefit to fill the resort with ticket buyers, no matter what they ride on. We all share the mountain and have a good time.

SKI SEASON, 1998–1999

We were looking for a repeat of the most recent season, but no such luck. It seemed like we just could not get two consecutive good snow years. When we would get a good one, it would be followed by two or three stinkers. This winter season was one of the latter. The Tahoe resorts were buried with heavier that average snow, but the storms tracked north of Sierra Summit. It hurt the important Christmas and New Year's holiday vacation season especially hard. Skiing was fair on man-made snow, but the good snow did not hit until mid-January. From then on, skiing was good on natural snow.

Sierra Summit started a new marketing program in February. They began selling season passes for the unheard of low price of $200.00; they were good for the balance of the 1999 season, and all of 1999–2000. This pass was good anytime: holidays, weekends, and weekdays. What a great deal for our local skiers! The plan really paid off for the resort. The first year, they sold 4000 passes, far beating the old sales of about 200. They now had loyal customers that could be counted on for the next season.

SUMMER, 1999

The pre-season sales of 4000 season passes at $200.00 each amounts to a nice chunk of cash to make summer improvements. The Day Lodge needed remodeling badly.

There was never enough room for people to come indoors during storms. They either stayed outdoors and got wet and cold, or packed up their kids in the car and headed home. This uncomfortable situation caused many skiers and boarders to stay away during storms. The planned Day Lodge addition would have added 8000 square feet to the food service area, the sport shop, the rental area, and the locker area. It was to be a wonderful improvement, but it was postponed.

Both back parking lots were graded and covered with asphalt, and that was another much needed improvement. They were only dirt before, and although they were fine when temperatures remained below freezing, they turned to mud as the days warmed up. The clearing of snow from these parking areas after heavy storms left chuck-holes the size of Volkswagens. Culverts were added to carry off the melt water to Big Creek.

The snowboard park was expanded to include more terrain features. A new run was converted to make more features, such as jumps and bumps.

Ullmann's Alley was named after the very popular and well-liked Walt Ullmann, who managed the sport shop for many years. Although Walt was involved in the sporting goods and ski-wear retail business for many years, he was not a skier. He was one of the very few long-time Sierra Summit employees who did not ski. He was around skiers day in and day out; he knew what ski-wear would sell, and what would not, yet he left the skiing to others. His name will remain with us as a permanent part of the mountain. This beautiful run named after Walt cuts off from Academy, makes a couple of sweeping turns, then joins back up with Academy, it is often carved and scooped to make dips and swoops enough to please the snowboarders. At other times, it can be peaceful and quiet. We have skied it hundreds of times, and thoughts of Walt were never far from our mind.

Here are Pete, the General Manager of Sierra Summit, and Walt Ullmann opening the new run that is primarily dedicated to snowboarders. Walt managed the sport shop at Sierra Summit for many years. He was one of the few management people at the resort who did not ski. He was around skiers daily and knew what they wanted and what would sell. *Photo courtesy the Scaparo collection.*

Walt died not long after he retired, and his long time assistant, Anita Lodge, stepped up to the task of managing the sport shop. Unlike Walt, Anita was an expert skier as well as an accomplisher marketer. Her artistic touch and knack for anticipating trends in ski fashion set the Sport Shop in a class all its own. The Sierra Summit Sport Shop carries clothing, goggles, sweaters, accessories, gifts and snacks.

SKI SEASON, 1999–2000

The season got off to a bad start due to lack of snow, thanks again to the La Nina weather pattern that had lingered much too long. The Christmas—New Year's holiday period was

Sport Shop Manager Anita's expertise in choosing just the right pants, sweaters, and accessories for the Sport Shop and the Fresno Store makes shopping almost as much fun as skiing. Her stores carry all the necessary fashions and gadgets that every skier needs to look and ski his best. Anita is an excellent skier.

once again nearly lost to skiing, with just a few runs open on man-made snow. As the new millennium approached, things got worse—a lot worse. Big Creek nearly stopped running, slowing to a trickle in December, shutting off the source of water for snowmaking. Big Creek is one of the sources of water for Huntington Lake, and it is fed by melting snow. There wasn't enough snow in the High Sierra from the previous years to provide enough water for snowmaking.

A desperate new supply was tried for the first time. The lake itself would have to become the water source. A ten-inch aluminum pipeline was laid to the lake, nearly a half-mile away, and a diesel-powered pump supplied the water for the snowmaking system. The pump ran for twenty-four hours a day for forty days. Crews stayed at the pump day and night to see that it was serviced. This made for a very expensive method to get water, but it worked. Natural snow fell in mid-January, but much of the season had been lost.

The younger skiers' and boarders' numbers were increasing, due to more runs catering just to boarders, jumpers, and rail-riders. The future in this resort business will certainly be determined by the youth of today. The baby boomers are aging and turning to other sports, or travelling to larger destination resorts. The final skier count for the season was a disappointing 100,000. Natural snowfall was just 240 inches.

SUMMER, 2000

The snowboard parks were very successful, and such a large attraction for the younger visitors, that the focus was now on increasing their capacity and hoping for a better year next year. With revenues down as much as they were for the last ski season, and the very expensive water-pumping operation that was required just to stay open, the money was very tight for this summer.

SKI SEASON, 2000–2001

For the second season in succession, Sierra Summit had a poor start, not receiving skiable natural snow until mid-January. The rule of thumb is that if the resort is not operational on natural or man-made snow for Christmas, the year will be a money-losing year. The holiday season makes all the difference in the world. Most years of the 1990s were profitable, but the last two were losers. Our local skiers expected to ski during their school vacations, but if that wasn't good, they would go to other resorts farther north. If they spent their ski money there, they did not have enough discretional money to ski at Sierra Summit. The early season pass sales are the main thing that kept them coming back. They had already paid for the pass, so they skied. The total skier visits were only 105,000. Only 5153 skiers visited in December, the lowest number since 1987.

General Manager Pete Scaparo and several of the key management people put together another plan to raise capital and purchase the resort. They outlined their plans to form a new corporation made up of employees and new investors, but again were unable to obtain the necessary funding, and the deal was never completed. The sale was not intended to be a takeover, as Snow Summit Ski Corporation had extended them an option to buy. The Snow Summit Ski Corporation was quick to add that they had not solicited a sale for the area, and they had no other purchasers in mind.

SUMMER, 2001

In August of 2001, Pete Scaparo gave his notice to resign as General Manager, a position that he had held for twenty years. Pete recommended his long-time assistant, Brian Bressel, to take over the job. Dick Kun, the corporate President,

Pete and Maureen Scaparo at their Fresno home in 2008.

reluctantly accepted Pete's resignation, and assigned Brian the position as the new General Manager. We hated to see Pete leave. He was the guy who could always be counted on to get things done. His wife, Maureen, was his secretary and his assistant. Most often, it was her voice who answered the telephones. The Scaparos are great people, and they had dedicated twenty years of their lives to making Sierra Summit what it is today. They were a very special family, an integral part of the mountain community. Their two daughters, Kim and Jennifer, grew up skiing the runs and working at the resort during the season. We wished them luck in their new endeavors, and bade them farewell. They would be missed.

SKI SEASON, 2001–2002

Brian Bressel got off to a great start! Finally, the Sierra Mountains had an early snow. It was early, and fell at just the

Father and son share a quiet moment on a sunny fall day while preparing for the 2008–2009 season. Brian Bressel has been the resort's general manager since 2001. Frank runs the Sierra Summit ski repair shop; he is the man to take your skis to for the yearly tune-up.

right times. The runs were well covered for the all important Christmas holidays. Maybe the new manager had a secret for bringing good snow. We hoped so. The early season set the tone for the entire season, and the skier count reflected that very well. Brian proved that he was up to the task, and has done a great job from the very first day.

The marketing was also starting to pay off. Many of the skiers came from not only the San Joaquin Valley, but from Bakersfield to the south, as well as the central coast areas of Santa Maria and San Luis Obispo. We were now seeing skiers from the Bay area and Monterey. Strong advertising in these areas was reaping profitable rewards. The youth market was growing as well. The popularity of the terrain parks and special promotions was growing incrementally. The season pass sales were at an all time high, with 5000 passes sold, good for the remainder of the year and all of the next year. The season ended with a whopping 142,000 skier visits and a record profit for the corporation.

SUMMER, 2002

With a profitable ski season the preceding winter, money was spent to beautify the area. Everything got a pretty coat of paint, and some buildings got new siding. Green and cream were the selected new colors, and up-to-date signs added to the fresh modern feeling.

SKI SEASON, 2002–2003

This was not the greatest for natural snow, but by Christmas the runs were covered, and that made all the difference between a good start and a poor start. Once a good, snowy holiday season is past the rest of the season just happens to follow along. The resort was in full operation during the Christmas-New Year's holiday. After December, the snowfall was sporadic, but skiable, thanks to great snowmaking to fill in the high traffic areas. The season lasted until April 27th. Season pass sales exceeded the last year, and the season ended with 142,000 skier visits. In the fall of 2002, the Snow Summit Ski Corporation bought another Southern California Ski Resort, Goldmine, adding their third ski resort to the California ski market. The name was changed to Bear Mountain.

SUMMER, 2003

The resort beautification program continued through the summer with the completion of the painting. There were no large projects started this year, even though the resort had a profitable ski season. Much work was going on at Bear Mountain, and some of the improvements that were planned for Sierra Summit would have to wait until the following summer.

SKI SEASON, 2003–2004

The drought continued in California. With help from snowmaking and enough natural snowfall, the Christmas

A new snow cover in December of 2007 is a welcome sight. This photo was taken from Chair #6 looking back to front entrance to the Inn.

holiday period was a success. The resort operated at full capacity with excellent business volume. Snowfall that continued through January and February kept the season rolling, although through the month of March, the weather was warm and dry. The season ended in March, with a skier visit total of 144,000. All in all, it was a successful year.

SUMMER, 2004

In the summer of 2004, Chair #6 was installed at the original location of the old Chair #1. The new lift terminated at Academy, delivering skiers to easy intermediate runs. Although the drive station, line equipment, and cable were new, the chairs had been used before. This lift also used the old lower bull-wheel terminal and the lower twelve towers from the original Chair #1. This additional lift would reduce

This chair serves beginner and intermediate runs, and was created out of the bottom half of the old Chair #1, which was decommissioned in 1991. The lower towers were left in place, as was the bull-wheel at the bottom. It was reconstructed in the summer of 2004 and renamed Chair #6.

This is the big circus-tent type structure on the east side of the base area near Chair #1. It was built in the summer of 2004 and enlarged by 50% a year later to house the bar and restaurant and provide much needed indoor seating during storms.

the waiting line on Chair #4 that also serves the new terrain park, built on Ridge Run. This hill is now mostly covered by snowmaking, and will be opening early in the season. Additional snow-making was added to Ridge Run.

Also new in 2004 was the 50' × 100' foot tent-like structure named Mainstream Station, offering food service, a bar, and much needed protection from storms. The fabric covered structure is on a cement floor, and is considered to be a permanent building. Outdoor seating and a patio area were installed at the same time. The total cost was about $100,000.

Sierra Summit's efforts to rebuild and improve the market in recent years with lower priced season passes, terrain parks, and other youth market incentives, and advertising in general, were paying off.

SKI SEASON, 2004–2005

The big news of the '04–'05 season is that we skied on Memorial Day weekend! This was the first time in Sierra

Summit history that this had happened. Not only was the ski season a late-closer, but it was also an early-opener, as well, which made for a great, long season. Wonderful early snows began arriving in late October, and with the help of snowmaking, allowed an opening day of November 6th. The snow pack continued to build, and skiing was great for the full year. Cold temperatures continued to work in the favor of the snowmakers. The good snow season dovetailed nicely with the improvements made during the summer, including the new Chair #6. The new Mainstream Station was proving to be very popular with the skiers, providing much needed additional food service and shelter during the storms. The eastern-most runs, Buckhorn, Dynamite, Grouse Creek, Waterfall, and Rancheria, all feed into the Station. The season ended with a skier visit total of 154,000. All in all, a very profitable year!

SUMMER, 2005

The new 2400-foot triple chairlift, Chair #7, was installed during the summer. It served the new runs on the west side, Westridge, Boonies, Ohana, and Lakeview. While it was called new, it was actually built up of mostly used parts, coming from Bear Mountain. Snow Summit Ski Corporation's other two resorts, Bear Mountain and Snow Summit, both have a higher traffic count than Sierra Summit, and they have replaced some of their lifts with newer high speed quads, sending the older equipment to Sierra Summit. This saved half the expense of a new lift, which would have cost about $900,000. The trades of equipment between the sister resorts allowed Sierra Summit access to equipment that the other resorts have outgrown, benefiting each, individually. This lift has the motor-drive unit at the base.

SKI SEASON, 2005–2006

Storm clouds began to gather early in the fall of 2005 as skiers and snowboarders danced snow dances and chanted snow prayers to the weather gods above. Prayers were answered generously, pleasing skiers, snowboarders, and ski-area managers as well. The season of 2005 started early, and by the Christmas holiday season, Sierra Summit was in full operation, with most runs adequately covered with natural snow, accentuated with man-made snow. The storms were well-timed so that they were spread out enough not to hinder automobile traffic and block weekend skiers.

Several of the improvements that were made during the past summer were very well received. The new Chair #7 on the west runs was definitely a winner. The newly opened runs that it served were very well appreciated, with many skiers heading directly to them for their first runs of the day. They were well-suited for intermediate and better skiers. The views were gorgeous and the skiers had the feeling of skiing on secluded runs that were free of the heavy traffic of Kaiser and Tamarack. The continued improvements to Sierra Summit did not go unnoticed; they pleased even the most discriminating skier. Mainstream Station was enlarged, adding about 50% to its capacity, with a neat deck space to enjoy a beer and a cheeseburger. You could kick back while watching the action on the newly-enlarged beginner slopes. A new belt lift (think of it as a moving sidewalk) made the uphill climb much easier for the new folks, whether big or little.

The skiing public responded to these great conditions by setting a record of 171,000 visits. This was the highest number ever for a season, and it also set a record for profit.

SKI SEASON, 2006–2007

How can we top a record-setting season like the last one? Well, to be perfectly blunt, we couldn't. We didn't even come close. The weather patterns continued to miss Sierra Summit in the late fall, and provided only sporadic snowfall in December. Once again, superb snowmaking ability and talented groomers rescued an otherwise poor start.

The natural snowfall continued through January, and we had good skiing on most of the runs. Those served by Chair #7 depended almost entirely of natural snow, but were adequately covered and offered good skiing. Skier visits for the year were 132,000, a little off the average, and far below the previous season.

SUMMER, 2007

The season received only about 50% of normal snowfall, once again pointing to the importance of snowmaking. It seems that no two years are alike. A pattern for one season certainly does not guarantee snowfall for the next. The all-important snowmaking capacity was improved during the summer by adding a second pump to augment the water flow volume out of Big Creek. A pump was also incorporated at Midway to provide more water flow uphill, and the storage pond above Midway was enlarged.

SKI SEASON, 2007–2008

A series of rather small storms in late November and early December, and expert snowmaking, allowed the resort to be open during the holiday season. This two-week season is so important; it seems to set the tone for the balance of the ski-months ahead. Skiers are a fickle bunch of people. They get in the habit of skiing every weekend, making for good skier visit counts, or they get turned-off early and pursue other hobbies. If the season starts with heavy snowfalls, some skiers tend to burn out early, but if the season is late in starting, the pent-up demand can provide good late season ski traffic.

The ski industry faces heavy competition in warm spring months when many skiers turn to boating, gardening, and other interests. It seems that if they get good skiing in the early season, they keep coming back. We saw plenty of happy skiers throughout the months of December and January; all lifts were open, and most runs were skiable.

The month of March brought an abrupt weather change to warmer and dryer conditions. Snowmaking was cranked up to near full capacity to keep slopes covered and maintain high skier-visits. Skier and snowboarders loved the sunny weather, but it took a lot of water to make enough snow.

The below average snowfall of the last two winters had failed to provide the high country with the snow-pack that is necessary to keep Big Creek flowing at a sufficient rate for snowmaking. The big pumps can suck more water out of the creek than it can produce. For only the second time in history, a pipeline was laid to Huntington Lake and water was pumped up to a small ponding area in the creek. This formed a holding basin to supply water for the pumps. This temporary holding system worked well and provided great skiing, but it was very expensive to operate. Skiers and snowboarders appreciated the effort to help Mother Nature, and the resort ended the season with a fairly good skier count of 151,000.

CHAPTER 9

The People Who Make Sierra Summit

THE SIERRA SUMMIT SKI PATROL

The Sierra Summit Ski Patrol was originally known as the China Peak Ski Patrol. The first group of patrollers at the new China Peak in 1958 came from the Fresno Ski Club. The Patrol was formed by Jack Pieroni, Yul Britton, Jim Adams, and Barbara Flint. They were there on opening day in 1958. As Jack explained to me, the first thing they had to do was attach yellow tape on trees to show skiers the easiest way down.

Fresno Bee writer Omer Crane covered the Fresno Ski Patrol at the opening of China Peak in an article on January 26, 1958. This is his article.

China Peak, Fresno County's new resort, is a superior testing ground for the patrol's skills, which it has acquired both on the slopes and in classes offered by the Fresno County Red Cross Chapter. The Fresno patrol also has a doctor-skier, in Dr. William Reynolds, a reassuring factor if there is a skier who needs reassurance.

We're doing what we can to make China Peak safe for all classes of skiers," says Yul Britton, the 26 year old head of the Fresno patrol. The Fresno unit has three paid skiers working full time Saturdays and Sundays at China Peak, and that number is supplemented by another dozen men and three or four women. Britton's chief aids at China Peak this winter are Bob Harris, Nip Ereman and alternate Bill Baker, who are paid by the resort.

The China Peak volunteer corps consists of Jim Bellinger, Herb Lange, Hal Larson, Don Little, Ted Miranda, Ralph

Dick Hudson and Jack and Lorraine Young follow Patrol Leader Fritz Mlekusch down Academy in early 1960s. *Photo courtesy Fritz Mlekusch collection.*

McElroy, Ralph Reed, Jack Pieroni, Tony Alfano, Larry Ecklund, Don Vest, and Ken Schroll. The girls are Lorraine Miranda, Peggy Case, and Pat Reed, whose assets are not altogether psychological.

This fine photograph depicts a training session in the 1960s. Assistant patrol leader Mel Meiklejohn, at right, watches as Fritz Mlekusch supervises a training session in moving an injured person. Don Code is standing at the left as Dick Hudson, Don Bright, and Jack and Lorraine Young are preparing the "injured person" for the sled ride downhill. *Photo courtesy Fritz Mlekusch collection.*

Another photo from the 1960s shows the China Peak Ski Patrol. From the left, Ricky Hudson, Lorraine Young, Fritz Mlekusch, Gwen Meiklejohn, Mel Meiklejohn, Dick Hudson, Don Bright, Don Code and Jack Young. *Photo courtesy Fritz Mlekusch collection.*

The article goes on to explain how an injured skier is wrapped in a blanket, taken down the hill in a "stretcher-toboggan," and once off the hill either Dr. Reynolds takes over or the casualty is taken to a doctor in Big Creek in a "Station Wagon-Ambulance."

The Ski Patrol matured quickly with the new resort, and it soon became a very important part of managing the mountain safely. The resort employed paid ski-patrollers, called Pro-Patrollers, and supplemented them with volunteers from the National Ski Patrol. The Pro-Patrollers after Yul Britton were Bob Harris, Nip Ereman and Bob Baker. Barbara Flint was the first National Ski Patrol leader; she had national number 122. Otto Tamm joined the Fresno Ski Patrol in 1958, and in 1960 he became the training and testing advisor. He was elected Patrol Leader in 1962. Otto is given the recognition he deserves in a later story. Look for it, because he has had such an important part in China Peak-Sierra Summit history.

One of the duties of the early day ski patrollers was making the snow safe to ski on. It was in drifts, tracks, bumps, and lumps, and packing the snow then was very crude by today's standards. One method of smoothing out the snow was with the Tucker Sno Cat. Without a doubt, these machines had limitations on where they could travel. Areas around loading the lifts and on steeper slopes were packed by side-stepping up and down the hill. (While the Tucker Sno Cat was a specific make of vehicle, we now refer to all snow-packing vehicles as snowcats. The snowcats now used at Sierra Summit are built by Bombardier.)

The Sierra Summit Ski Patrol has grown with the ski resort, under the dedicated leadership of such people as Larry Ecklund, Otto Tamm, Fritz Mlekusch, and Bill Littleton. It has grown to become one of the finest patrols in the far west. In the 1969 season, the patrol had 68 members, and the patrol volunteered 1238 ski-days.

The Sierra Summit Ski Patrol for the 2006–2007 ski season poses for a group photo during the annual ski patrol refresher. All patrollers must attend the refresher at the beginning of the season to be eligible to patrol. Here they learn the latest techniques of first-aid, are tested on their skills, and recertify winter emergency first aid certification. *Photo courtesy Michael Nolen collection.*

Don Harmon joined the National Ski Patrol as a candidate in 1969, and he soon became a qualified patroller. He went on to become the director of the Pro Patrol in 1972, and served for five years. He was followed by Larry Thomas, Rich Bailey, Matt Conley, Bo Yule, and Mike Nolen.

One day in January of 1969, the patrol was put to their toughest test up to that time. About 3:00 P.M., Chair #1 broke down and stopped, due to an electrical failure. It stranded all skiers riding on the lift, for only the second time in its history (the first time was Thanksgiving Day, 1967). The ski patrol on duty that day was made up of Pro Patrollers and National volunteers, and they had everyone safely off the lift by 3:45. This was not an easy task, because in many places the chairs are more than thirty feet in the air.

Evacuation of a chairlift is accomplished by sending a rope over the cable supporting the chairs by first shooting a lead fishing sinker attached to a monofilament line over the cable with a sling-shot. Then, a heavier rope is attached to the fishing line, and it is pulled up and over the cable. A canvas sling is pulled up to the chair passenger, and he is instructed to pull it on like a bosun's seat. He then pushes himself clear of the chair and is lowered to the surface by two patrollers standing on the ground, belaying the rope and counterbalancing his weight. Each passenger is instructed to keep his skis on while he is being lowered. He is then unloaded individually, with teams starting at the top of the lift-line and at the bottom. The longest lift at Sierra Summit can be evacuated in forty-five minutes.

By 1970, the Fresno Ski Patrol had grown to 89 regular members, nine junior members, and eleven auxiliaries, according to a *Fresno Bee* article on Sunday, December 13, 1970, written by Fritz Mlekusch, a China Peak Ski Patroller. Fritz is one of the most interesting skiers that I've interviewed for my research. He was born in Austria, and when the Germans invaded his homeland, he was put into a Prisoner of War camp at age thirteen. After immigrating to the United States with his Russian-born wife, Kitty, he became a mechanic at a Fresno Volkswagen dealer. He always had a new VW to drive skiing, and invented a modification to lock one rear wheel if it was spinning in snow, transferring power to the other wheel. Fritz was also president of the Fresno Ski Club in 1964–1965. The Fresno Ski Club and the China Peak-Sierra Summit Ski Patrol had many common members. Both were important to Sierra Summit history. Fritz was in charge of training new patrollers and candidates, and as he related to me in our interview, he ran a very tight ship. Pictures and stories certainly validated his claim. Fritz insisted that every patroller have a warm up before starting the patrol day. They were instructed to follow him up the lift line, under Chair #1, to tower 12, which was halfway to the top. This climb was done on skis and on snow, with a combination of herringbone steps and traversing. He also inspected every patroller's fanny pack before allowing them to patrol for the day. At that time, China Peak was required to have nineteen patrollers on the hill on a weekend, and Fritz telephoned the members on Friday night to be sure he would have the required number for Saturday and Sunday.

There are patrollers on the hill any time the resort is open, in all weather, from lift opening until long after closing, ensuring every skier is off the mountain safely. The Forest Service requires one paid patroller to be on the hill for every lift that is operating. The patrol's mission is skier safety and that has never changed. It has become increasingly more important. The word "skier" in this case should be changed to "guest," as this encompasses boarders, snowshoers, picnickers, and hotel guests. Sometimes, patrollers are called upon to render first aid to non-skiers, and many times in the past

Fritz at his Fresno home, summer, 2008.

Dick Hudson, an early-day China Peak ski patrolman, is still active in all mountain sports, hiking bicycle riding and skiing. Many of the black and white early-day photographs are from his collection.

they have responded to automobile accidents near the resort. On various occasions, they have conducted searches for lost people. The work of the patroller is changing with the times. In the past, there had been a definite distinction between the Pro Patrollers, who were paid, and the National Ski Patrollers, who were all volunteers. The uniforms were distinctively different, and attitudes sometimes reflected this difference as well. The Pros tended to be younger. They were full time skiers and better at the craft than the volunteers, most of whom had to earn their living at a "real" job. The differences are blurring now, as many of the Pros are older, and we even see some retirees patrolling. As the patrollers leave the first-aid room to start their day, they are all equal; they now wear the same uniform and share the same duties.

Patrollers are reminded that they are, in many ways, representing the resort, and the guests are to be treated respectfully and courteously. Their safety and enjoyment are equally

Larry Thomas, pro patrol leader from 1974 to 1983, poses with his staff: Larry Thomas, Chuck Dodds, Mike Arnold, George Fox, Rich Bailey, Barry Smith, Don Harmon, and Bernard Scherrer. *Photo courtesy Rich Bailey collection.*

Rich Bailey became pro patrol leader in 1983, and served until 1987. Here the group stops for a portrait in front of the old First Aid room on the ground floor of the day lodge. From left is Mike Arnold, Brian Chenault, Don Harmon, Larry Thomas, Rich Bailey, Chuck Dodds, Bernard Scherrer and Barry Smith. *Photo courtesy Rich Bailey collection.*

important to their choice of a ski resort. The patrol is also responsible for investigating accidents and interviewing witnesses, which is an important part of determining the cause of an accident. Even the name, Sierra Summit Ski Patrol, which has demanded respect for 28 years, has been changed to High Sierra Ski Patrol, Sierra Summit.

The High Sierra Ski Patrol suffered a great loss on Friday morning, September 29, 2006. Long-time National Patroller, John Jamison, and his two adult sons, Sean and Bryan, were killed in an early morning car accident in Northern California. At the Sierra Summit Patrol Awards Banquet earlier in the year, on May 12, 2006, John had been honored for 37 years of outstanding leadership to both the National Ski Patrol and the Sierra Summit Ski Patrol. John was also honored for four years as Volunteer Patrol Coordinator. He will be sorely missed by his family of fellow patrollers.

MICHAEL NOLEN

Mike Nolen, the patrol director, started his long career with Sierra Summit in November, 1984, as a Professional Patrol Trainee, and was "crossed" (awarded the cross on the back of his jacket) as a Professional Patroller the same season. Mike was promoted to Patrol Supervisor in 1987 and Director in 1990. Mike oversees about twenty paid patrollers, and approximately 120 volunteers. He was named National Outstanding Professional Patroller of the United States by the National Ski Patrol, and was the winner of the Gold Star. Mike also serves as Certified Supervisor of the Far West Division of the National Ski Patrol. These are very prestigious awards, and Sierra Summit is indeed fortunate to have people of his caliber on their staff.

Many of Sierra Summit's long-time employees work year-round keeping up with resort maintenance. However, Mike has a separate career with the U.S. Forest Service as Lead Wilderness Ranger. I asked him if his responsibilities with

Here Mike Nolen, the ski patrol director, takes a moment to give his hard working helper—trained search and rescue dog Brika—a well-deserved pat on the head. *Photo courtesy Michael Nolen collection.*

the Forest Service conflicted in any way with his role at Sierra Summit, which is on land leased under special permit from the Forest Service. He assured me that there were no conflicts. Mike has managed a number of timber sales around the Sierra Summit Mountain Resort, and within their permit area. His most recent project, as the lead from the Forest Service perspective, was the expansion of Chair #7, East Bowl, Waterfall Bowl, and some powder chutes.

RICH BAILEY

Sierra Summit is very fortunate to have key employees who remain for many years. The lessons that are learned at this mountain resort are valuable, and although some are easily transferable to another mountain resort, many are unique. No two mountains are the same. Each has different

Mountain Manager Rich, as he is known to everyone—his real name is Richard—is truly dedicated to the sport of skiing. His job encompasses all aspects of mountain operations, from grooming to snow making. He is a full time employee and spends the summers preparing the runs and seeing that improvements are made, whether it means moving boulders or cutting twigs and brush. Rich is a licensed blaster, and is responsible for avalanche control.

terrain, slopes, and drainages. Mountains have personalities that must be understood by folks who tread on them. Weather patterns that favor one mountain may be treacherous on another. Rich Bailey is a man who knows Sierra Summit as intimately as any dangerous mistress.

Richard Bailey has a B.S. degree in Resource Management from Cal Poly, San Luis Obispo, so his credentials are formal as well as learned by experience. Rich began his long career with China Peak as a National Ski Patroller in 1972, and turned Pro in the following year. Rich became the Pro Patrol leader in 1983 and continued until 1987, when he was promoted to Mountain Manager. Rich is still a patroller, but his additional managerial duties include the snowmaking division, the snow-grooming division, and the avalanche control specialists. In addition to numerous ski patrol-related credentials, such as Emergency Medical Technician and Red Cross Emergency Response Instructor, Rich is licensed by the California Division of Occupational Safety and Health as an Explosive Blaster for avalanche control and construction. In the summer, he uses his blasting skills to clear boulders and rocks from runs.

Rich Bailey shows the experts how it's done in this great deep-powder shot. All three skiers are displaying perfect form for blasting through the deep stuff. Behind Rich Baily is Spencer Neville and Lorre Mock. *Photo courtesy the Rich Bailey collection.*

WHAT MAKES SNOW?

Since the mountain manager is responsible for the conditions on the mountain, now might be the proper time to explain some of the requirements for good skiing conditions. First, let's look at the term "man-made snow." This is real snow; it's just as real as any God-given snow. It is produced by pumping a water spray into the air at high pressure, during sub-freezing temperatures. The colder the temperature, the better the system works because it freezes sooner. With more than twenty years' experience, Sierra Summit crews have become experts at knowing when conditions are optimal for snowmaking. As the years have passed since that first machine was introduced in 1977, many improvements have been added.

Permanent above-ground plumbing has now been installed on most of the mountain. This requires two pipes, one for water, and one for compressed air. The compressed air is produced by a high volume compressor near the base.

Another lonely gun working hard to keep Express covered with fresh powder near the unloading ramp of Chair #6.

Sierra operates eight of these portable blowers in addition to the permanent guns. This unit uses water from the permanent pipes to spray mist into turbines driven by an electric motor. You will often see these machines working where needed to provide supplementary coverage. There will probably be a diesel powered generator running nearby to provide 440 volt AC power.

The water is taken out of Big Creek by powerful pumps and sent through the plumbing up the mountain. There are hydrants at strategic locations near the runs where hoses connect to guns. The guns have nozzles at their tips which mix the water and air. It is this mixture that produces the snow. It is then sprayed in the desired direction. In addition to the snow guns are eight Lenko portable units. These are huge turbine-type fans driven by a powerful electric motor. They use water supplied by the fixed pipelines, but provide their own air. The motors are powered by long 440-volt extension cords or by portable diesel generators. They can be moved wherever they are needed.

Since the temperatures fall after sundown, much of the snowmaking is done by the night crews. Snowcats towing grooming equipment smooth out and spread snow where it is needed. When the runs are opened to the first skiers in the early morning hours, perfect conditions welcome the early guests. Another benefit from nighttime snowmaking is that the noise of snow guns is usually finished by daybreak, leaving peaceful soft white snow. Oftentimes, skiers see snowmaking guns running during the day. They are making snow on runs that are not open to skiing. Like fishing, the best conditions are enjoyed by the early risers; late sleepers just don't know what they are missing!

Today, probably no ski area in California could exist without snowmaking. It's part of the cost of doing business. Snowmaking is not only used in the early season when no storms are occurring, but they are used pretty much all during the season to cover high traffic areas. These are areas where snow gets worn out by many skiers, near loading ramps, ticket areas, and food service sites.

Many terms have evolved over the years to describe snow conditions. Perhaps a glossary is in order, starting with the best conditions:

1. **Fresh powder**. This is what the experts pray for. It's not easy to ski; it takes years of practice, and strong legs, but once you get good at it, you can't help but love it. Off the runs and through the trees—man, this is snow to die for. It's best during storms. That's why we ski when the softies are sleeping late.
2. **Packed powder**. This is much easier to ski. It's soft snow that has been packed by a snowcat. Any intermediate skier can ski this: It's so easy we call it "hero" snow, because it makes everybody ski like a hero.
3. **Packed snow**. No mention of powder gives snow condition away. It's harder, faster, and requires more edging.
4. **Crud**. A mixture of every kind of snow, good skiers learn to handle this easily, but it is definitely not good for beginners.

5. **Hard pack.** This is just a nice word for hard frozen snow. It is not ice, but almost as hard. Caution is definitely advised here.

6. **Corduroy.** This is soft snow that was just packed by a snowcat. This is so cool to ski on that it makes everybody look like an expert. It disappears quickly as more skiers pass over it.

This beautiful photo shows the ski school's red sweaters, which were in use from 1970 to 1973. It was always necessary for the ski instructors to be immediately identifiable on the hill. They were looked up to by the customers, and referred to as ski gods; a term that the ski school did little to change.

This group of instructors includes: Ski School Director Phil Kerridge, Dick Shimizu, Otto Tamm, Bob Zakarian, George Kinney, Scott McLagan, Assistant Director Alan Shimizu, Rick Hudson, Skip Bullock, Roger Coats, Sandy Kerridge, Stephanie McLagan, Dan Clack, Steve Thompson, Kathy Clack, Melody Kinney, and Helen Amerine. Several of the instructors are not identified. *Photo courtesy Phil Kerridge collection.*

This is the same group of instructors, but from a slightly different angle. The photo was taken on the bunny hill, between the rope tow, and Chair #3, before the hill was recontoured. It was referred to then as "Thunder Mountain." The rope tow is visible above the heads of the instructors. Please note the automobile wheel on the pole that supports the downhill rope. The rope that traveled uphil dragged along in the snow, staying soaking wet and cold until a skier picked it up for the pull up the hill. This tow was powered by a trusty Ford V8 60 horsepower automobile engine, and was very difficult to use, especially for beginners. *Photo courtesy Phil Kerridge collection.*

SIERRA SUMMIT SKI SCHOOL

It would be hard to pick a department of a ski resort that is the most important to that resort's growth and the growth of future ski business. What department contributes the most significant functions to guarantee that new skiers are joining the sport? New skiers are needed to replace the older generation that simply wears out or turns to another hobby. For any sport to flourish and grow there must be a constant influx of newcomers to be introduced and taught the complexities that the more experienced have mastered.

Ski schools have been a part of the scene since the very first days of skiing in Europe. The methods pioneered by the Swiss and Austrians are the basis for teaching skiing in the United States today. The Tenth Mountain Division of the U.S.

Along with the name change from China Peak to Sierra Summit, the school got brand new uniforms. This group of instructors include: Ron Mitchell, Linda Robertson, Gerald Mele, Patty Paulson, Martha Porter, Jane Mele, Kate McBride, Terry Taylor, Kelly Spickler, Kris Spickler, Mallory Hawkins, Skip Bullock, John Edwards, Roger Boos, Steve Manfredo, Roger Coats, Jim Benelli, Phil Kerridge, Wayne Cook, Mark Henry, John Dark, Mark Coleman, Robin Dark, Lisa Anderson, Lorre Mock, Janet Bauer, Danny Fletcher, Mike Reilly, Neal Jennings, Todd Hendrickson, Grant Seals, Robin Dark, Eric Tobias, Tom Locker and Spencer NeVille. Not shown are some long time instructors, Dr. Jim Walters, Bob Soares, Walt Wasser, and others.

Army Ski Troops trained near Aspen during WWII. Since there were very few trained ski instructors in the U.S. at the time, instructors were recruited from Europe. At the end of World War II, many of these European instructors stayed in the U.S. and were instrumental in designing and building the American ski resorts. Their teaching methods were taught to American ski instructors, and the basics remained the same. The Europeans demanded complete discipline in their instructors, and the instructors commanded respect from their students. Along with the basic principles of the

Arlberg Method, the etiquette of skiing was also emphasized. Skiing was not a sport that could be learned from watching the expert schuss by at full speed. The basics of the sport must be understood before one can ski safely.

Sierra Summit, and before it, China Peak, is situated in the Sierra National Forest, and has been granted permission to operate a ski resort, providing certain prerequisites are met. One requirement is for the resort to have a fully staffed ski school, under the direction of a Certified Ski Instructor. From the opening day until now, Sierra Summit has operated an exceptional ski school with professional instructors.

Phil was the new ski school director, starting in 1968. *Photo courtesy the Kerridge collection.*

Phil is showing his excellent ability here, blasting his way through deep powder. *Photo courtesy Phil Kerridge collection.*

China Peak's first ski school director was Bud Nillson, originally from Sweden. He stayed until the spring of 1962. Some of Bud's first instructors were Joe Senglaub and Joanne Senglaub, and Ed and Lois Seigle. The ski school staff grew with weekend instructors Walt McMullen, Del LaFace, Norm Clark, George Kamienski, and Tony Alfano. Racing Coach Ray Kellner formed the China Peak racing team. Otto Tamm was another early ski instructor, at times serving as ski school director while the resort was mired in the bankruptcy troubles in the early sixties. In 1964, the resort's new general manager, Don Redmond, announced that Bob Autry, assistant coach to Dave McCoy's race team at Mammoth, would be the new China Peak Ski School director. Bob stayed four years and was replaced by Phil Kerridge.

When Phil was promoted to a management position in 1985, he was followed by Gary Forrest for the 1986–1987 season, Gerald Wallace for the 1988–1989 season, and then

Colin Baldock. Colin left in 2002 to take over the Yosemite Ski School, and the directorship was passed to Jennifer Gray. Her story will come up later.

PHIL KERRIDGE

Phil has been an employee of China Peak-Sierra Summit since 1968. That makes him the longest-term employee, with

Phil was ski school director and Frances was ski shool supervisor during this time. *Photo courtesy Phil Kerridge collection.*

more than forty years with the company. In the ski industry, which is known for a high turnover, he is unique.

Phil grew up in southern California, getting his first taste of skiing by joining the Fullerton High School ski club, which was probably the first high school to have a ski club. As soon as he was old enough to drive, he had a way to get to the ski areas on his own. He attended Fullerton City College for two years, and skied every vacation. Phil graduated from University of Redlands with a BS degree in geology. His first job was with Union Oil as a paleontologist, but didn't like the confines of an office. There were not many jobs available, so he joined the Naval Air Reserve and became a flight crew member as a radar officer on P2–V aircraft. He was also interested in flying, and had earned his private pilot's license in high school.

In 1960, he went to Mammoth and joined the ski patrol. Although he felt he was not the greatest skier, he took every opportunity to ski with the pros at Mammoth Ski School. He applied for, and was hired as a ski instructor. This led to a six-year stay at Mammoth.

Phil worked with many great skiers and was eager to learn from them. One was Deklan Daley, who had trained in France. Mammoth was teaching the rotation method, but France was teaching a modified technique, and that seemed to make learning easier. Deklan felt that the Americans were better teachers, but could learn a great deal from the French.

In 1967, P.S.I.A. (the Professional Ski Instructors of America) sponsored Phil to go to France to train with the French National Ski School. Phil graduated second in his class, missing first place only because he did not speak French. When he returned to Mammoth, he was named Assistant Ski School Director. From Mammoth, Phil was hired as Ski School Director at Mt. Ashland, Oregon, for the 1967–68 season.

Phil was hired in 1968 to be the new ski school director at China Peak. Joanne Weirick had worked with Phil at Mammoth, knew his dedication to teaching, and felt he would be an asset to China Peak. She invited him to come take a look. Phil liked the new area, and took the job. He was well received, and he did a great job of building the school. Phil ushered in a new era in the ski school, adding two French instructors, Denys Liboz and Alan Betrand. In addition to his ski school duties, Phil worked with Ray Kellner and Stan Beach to build the race team. Phil was named a junior examiner by the P.S.I.A. in 1964, and was named senior examiner from 1965 until 1968. The P.S.I.A. is responsible for testing and certifying ski instructors. In 1986, the P.S.I.A. made him a lifetime member. Phil was responsible for having the race course at China Peak U.S.S.A. and F.I.S. certified.

Phil left the ski school in 1985, looking for a change, as he needed new challenges. By this time, Sierra Summit (the name changed in 1982) needed a chief electrician.

Ski areas run on electricity, lots of it, and some is very high voltage. Phil was awarded the responsibility for not only maintaining the equipment, but planning for the expansion that was sure to follow, as the new owners had great future plans. New technology was evolving in communications equipment, the PBX system, credit card system, web cams, television, and satellite systems. In addition to Phil's new responsibilities, he developed and managed the Employee Skier Safety Program, and was the coordinator for the Sierra Summit Race Team. Phil is still employed at Sierra Summit, and at this writing, has been with the resort longer than any other employee—more than forty years!

THE FRESNO SKI CLUB

The oldest ski-club in central California is the Fresno Ski Club. During the late 1930s and early 1940s, the *Fresno Bee* published a series of articles about skiing and winter sports by Christie Slalom (yes, that is the author's name). This article appeared on the sports page, January 26, 1940.

The Fresno Ski Club, which has a membership of about 300, was formed early in 1934 with eleven charter members. John Cooper, Fresno department store executive, was the first president of the organization and had been active in promoting the extensive programs of the club.

The first major activity of the group was a ski trek into the backcountry of the Sierra by three members who were seeking the site of a lodge on Kaiser Peak. Cooper, Dick Mitchell and John Hodgkin made the journey, fought through a blinding snowstorm and finally reached the peak where they signed the register and then began the arduous trip back.

Late in 1935 the club started a series of educational pro-grams and instructions for tyros. Films of skiing trips were displayed and new members were taught the fine art of handling their runners.

The club also has a dormitory at Fish Camp where approximately 100 winter sports adherents can be accommodated. There is a 1,500 foot ski tow, several fine runs and ice skating rinks there.

WE'RE A SKI CLUB—PLUS A WHOLE LOT MORE!

The following is reprinted with permission from The Fresno Ski Club Website:

The Fresno Ski Club is made up of a diverse group of individuals that have a few things in common. First is a thirst for outdoor alpine activity. Whether it's making the short trek to see our friends at Sierra Summit, getting off to a weekender in Tahoe, or spending an entire week taking in everything a world class ski resort in Utah, Colorado, Oregon, Canada, etc., has to offer; members of the Fresno Ski Club crave to go wherever there is an opportunity for fresh tracks and fun in the snow.

When the snow melts, these same crazed folks are often seen hiking, biking, boating, or perhaps taking in the opening of a local art show, concert, or paying a visit to a winery. The Ski Club is a social organization that gives every member the opportunity to participate in organized outings the year around.

Another common trait within the group is a bit of wanderlust. Call it a love for travel. Every winter, we organize at least three or four trips to Tahoe that leave late Friday afternoon and return Sunday evening. We have at least three longer, out-of-state trips each winter. Occasionally, a European or international vacation is thrown in for the truly insane, or the wonderfully sane, depending on your perspective. Yes, there's something for everyone. Some members, after skiing together for years, or in some cases having barely met, have ventured off on their own trips, with as few as a couple, or as many as thirty people, from both within and out of the club. Those madcap mavericks!

Throughout its history, the Fresno Ski Club has been a source for meeting people with like interests, varied as they may be, with resulting friendships, social contacts, and lifelong partnerships formed on an ongoing basis. It's a friendly group. All skill levels of skiers and snowboarders are to be found within the club, from the beginner novice to the highly skilled experts. Some members are just learning the basics, while others may be relearning those skills which have lain dormant for a year or two, or three, or ten. There is no need to by shy, even if you have forgotten how to snowplow! There are plenty of resident expertise you can observe, emulate, and from which you will ultimately learn.

At one time, the Fresno Ski Club even considered owning its own resort. In an article published in the *Fresno Bee*, dated February 10, 1946, the Fresno Ski Club is listed as one of the parties interested in developing a ski resort in the Sierra. The club did not pursue the Forest Service Permit seriously, and the final bid went to Knute Flint to develop China Peak.

THE ESTONIANS

Sierra Summit, and before that, China Peak, has played host to many ski clubs—some are old and some not so old. Some start up, last a few years, and fizzle like melting snow. The Estonian Ski Club is one of the oldest, second only to the Fresno Ski Club. This last winter, the club made their forty-seventh annual ski trip to Sierra Summit. The club calls Southern California home, but the members of Estonian descent come from all over the Western United States.

The club started its annual trek to China Peak at the invitation of Otto Tamm, a popular ski instructor and ski patroller of the early days of the resort. He invited a few of his Estonian friends to come ski with him, and they haven't stopped

March 2008 found the Estonian Ski Club enjoying their forty-first annual visit to Sierra Summit. The last day of their visit is dress-up day, and a wonderful day for photography. All the adults ski in formals and tuxedos. The kids dress up, too; nobody is left out.

The whole group gathers in front of the bull-wheel of Chair #6 for their group portrait on March 9, 2008. This is a group of happy, fun-loving expert skiers. They started skiing at China Peak when Otto Tamm, the legendary ski instructor and patroller, invited a few of his Estonian friends form southern California to come up and ski with him. They have been coming every winter since from all over the western United States to enjoy the hospitality of Sierra Summit.

coming since. The whole club meets at Sierra Summit each spring. Every year, between 100 and 200 faithful members make their annual visit. This usually fills the small hotel to capacity, and at times, they have even been known to sleep in the hallways. It has been rumored that, on occasion, they have emptied every bottle in the bar, but this has never been proved or disproved.

The local skiers look forward to the yearly visit of the Estonians. They have a well-earned reputation of fun-loving parties, good times, and expert skiing. For some, this is a great time to meet friends, both old and new. The most colorful event of their visit is dress-up day, on the last Sunday of their visit, when they ski in formal attire. Yes, the ladies wear real formals, and tuxedos for the men. This is a family affair

The Estonian Ski Club is made of people of Estonian descent from the western United States. They have been skiing at China Peak/Sierra Summit yearly for more that forty years. The club has no rules or requirements, except that everybody have a good time. They descend on the resort for a week at a time, with 100 or more happy skiers. On the last day of their visit they ski in formals, tuxedos and funny costumes. This colorful event is a favorite among the local skiers, and is a real "Kodak Moment," and photographers are welcome.

and kids dress up in crazy costumes, too. The reason for this crazy get-up was explained like this:

"Many of our Estonian friends are college graduates, and belonged to fraternities, sororities, and professional clubs that held regular off-campus meetings. While attending these social meetings, all members wore formal attire. So, as the logic goes, this ski weekend is really just another social get-together, so why not dress accordingly?"

Makes sense to me. Where else do you see expert skiers bombing the steepest slopes with crinoline petticoats and black swallow tails flapping in the wind? These are Kodak moments of the highest order, and everybody poses for group pictures before retiring to the bar or sundeck.

Where did Estonians come from? What possible thread does a group of people have in common that has brought them back to Sierra Summit yearly for forty-two years? Estonia is a very small country that is nestled between Finland on the north, Russia on the east, and Latvia to the south. Although it is near the Arctic Circle, it enjoys a mild climate, due to the Atlantic currents. What Estonia hasn't enjoyed very much of is freedom. It has been ruled by Russian Czarists, the Russians, the Germans, and then, the Russians again. It is finally free, due to the breakup of the U.S.S.R. The end of WWII gave many of her people a chance to escape the chaos. Many of them came to the U.S. and settled in the western states. The Estonian people have a great love for their mother country and try to keep the customs and language alive. As the original immigrants get older, more and more children and grandchildren are coming to ski Sierra Summit.

OTTO TAMM

Otto Tamm is the reason behind the Estonian Ski Club, and it is because of him that the club skis at Sierra Summit. He is an important figure in area skiing and in the history of the resort; his past is fascinating, filled with intrigue, and it needs to be told. Otto was a man who left a lasting legacy on every trail of snow that he ever skied, from his native Estonia to China Peak. Many people have left their mark, but none is more indelible than Otto's. His wonderful legend still lives through his daughters Kati and Tiina.

Otto joined the Fresno Ski Patrol in 1958, and shared the duties of ski patroller and ski instructor. He was an instructor first, but he will be remembered most for his contributions to the ski patrol. He was a likeable man, gifted with great ski ability, and was a wonderful teacher. He was always willing to help a skier in need. An energetic person, he possessed the work ethic of his native country, not to mention its accent. "Ya, dat iss good," he would say, with his infectious smile. Otto's native language was Estonian, but he was also fluent in German, Russian, and Finnish. When a happy grin crossed

This family has had a lasting impact on the Sierra Summit resort. Otto is shown here wearing his ski patrol uniform, with his wife Reeta and daughters Tiina and Kati. Otto was a ski instructor and the ski school director before becoming ski patrol leader. Tiina and Kati grew up to become top racers. It was Otto who was responsible for starting the Estonian Ski Club, made up of his friends from Estonia who came to China Peak to ski. Now, after more than forty years, the Estonian Ski Club visit is a yearly event. It is colorful, lighthearted, and fun for everyone. *Photo courtesy the Tamm Family Collection.*

his face, it slightly exposing his lower teeth, showing a slight under bite. He was older than most of the other instructors. He was in his mid-forties at the time, and his receding hairline quickly set him apart from the others. It has been said that ski instructors skied hard all day and partied heavily at night. Well, not quite true, at least not for Otto. Family life played an important part in Otto's life. His wife, Reeta, sold lift tickets, and his two daughters were never far away when the family worked on weekends.

Born on February 22, 1915, in Pskov, Russia, his family fled over the border to escape World War I, and Otto spent

Kati spent her childhood years skiing China Peak/Sierra Summit at every opportunity. Under the watchful eye of her famous father, she grew into an outstanding racer, winning events all over the western United States. She worked many years as an instructor, and now is an active member of the Estonian Ski Club, and makes her way from her home in Portland often to enjoy Sierra Summit.

his childhood years in Petseri. He was active in sports as a youngster, with skiing and bicycling his best sports. In 1939, at the age of sixteen, he represented Petseri's Home Guard at the Estonian National Ski Championships, and finished sixth in the 10K cross-country. At the Estonian National Ski Championships in 1935, he came in first in ski jumping and the combined 18K cross-country and jumping. In 1938, he again placed first in this event. He attended and graduated from the Finnish Sports Academy in Lahti, Finland, specializing in cross-country and jumping. He joined the Estonian Calvary because they had a skier–bicycle squadron. From there, he was sent to military school for officer training, and graduated a Lieutenant Jr. grade. He was accepted into the Estonian Air Force and trained as a pilot. He became a fighter pilot, displaying his extreme athletic ability and split second timing, honed by years of skiing

Tiina grew up in a family of outstanding skiers, and true to the family tradition, became a champion racer, competing in many events against her older sister Kati. These sisters could often be counted on to finish in first and second place, determined only by who had the best luck on a given day. Their father, Otto, was their coach, and he demanded excellence in their performance. Like her sister Kati, Tiina worked many years as an instructor at China Peak/Sierra Summit.

competition. The Estonians were trying to keep the Russians in their place and protect their tiny homeland.

Estonia had enjoyed only twenty years of independence from Czarist Russia when Josef Stalin laid claim to the nation in 1940. During the Nazi thrust toward Moscow in World War II, the Soviets were forced east and Estonia came under German domination. The Estonian pilots were offered the choice of commissions in the Luftwaffe, or death by firing squad. Otto made the first choice to fight against the Soviets. He flew 61 low-level bombing missions over Russia, and was shot down once. When the Russians again took over Estonia, he flew his German Focker–Wulf 190 fighter west into the American Zone of West Germany and surrendered. He felt this was his best chance of survival, as the Russians would have sent him to a Siberian slave labor camp if they captured him. He wound up teaching skiing to American GIs at Garmish–Partenkirchen, a ski resort in Germany, after the war ended in 1945. He had made the right choice! His wife followed him to West Germany, and in 1950 they were permitted into the U.S. (This history is compiled from two *Fresno Bee* articles, dated Sunday, Feb. 7, 1960, by Omer Crane, and the second, dated Sunday, Mar. 4, 1990, by Lois Henry.)

Otto chose Fresno as a good place to settle and raise his family, consisting of his wife, Reeta, and daughters, Kati and Tiina. The dominant ski-gene was passed on to the girls; it would only grow to enrich their lives, just as it had Otto's. Skiing had always been his passion, but that did little to pay the bills in the long hot Fresno summers, so he started painting houses, and soon had a thriving painting business.

In China Peak's first year, 1958, Otto joined the small Fresno Ski Patrol. In 1959, he was named Course Setter Official, preparing for the 1960 Squaw Valley Winter Olympics. By the winter of 1960, Otto was named Training and Testing Advisor for the California Central Region of the National Ski Patrol. In the winter of 1964, Otto was named head of China Peak Ski School, a position he held in addition to patrol leader of the Fresno Ski Patrol. The Fresno Patrol was Otto's first love, but coaching the racing team and training kids were important, too. He had organized the first junior ski patrol in 1961. The uniform he designed for the Fresno chapter was adopted as the official uniform by the National Board and became the standard for the country. The Fresno Ski Patrol, under Otto's leadership, was one of the best in the western states. He was elected Regional Director in 1968, '69, and '70.

Otto was active in his later years. He enjoyed the fruits of his labors, and watched his daughters win race after race. Kati and Tiina followed in their father's boot print and both were ski instructors at Sierra Summit, and are now active in the Estonian Ski Club. Otto died in 1998.

Jack Pieroni has probably done more to promote the sports of skiing and snowboarding than any one person in Fresno County. He skied at China Peak on its opening day in 1958, and has never stopped. He sells skis all week at Herb Bauer's and skis every Sunday during the season. If you bought skis in Fresno in the last fifty years, chances are good that you probably bought them from Jack.

JACK PIERONI

Jack Pieroni has been selling skis, boots, and equipment in the Fresno area for more than fifty years, so if you bought skis in the last half century, they probably came from Jack. No one person has done more to promote our sport than Jack, not only in the ski business, but through the Fresno Ski Patrol, of which he was a founding member, and the Fresno Ski Club. The Ski Patrol was actually formed inside the

Fresno Ski Club. Jack was a very active member of the Fresno Ski Club for many years.

Jack was at China Peak on opening day, and that alone makes him special. On that day in 1958, he and fellow patrollers, Yul Britten and Jim Adams, attached yellow tape to trees to show skiers the easiest way down the mountain.

Jack caught the ski bug early in life. He was a boy scout, and went with his troop to Yosemite's Badger Pass during the days when they had a giant sled which hauled skiers up the hill. They referred to this wonderful invention as the "Queen Mary."

A Fresno native, Jack attended Fresno High School and Fresno State College. When Jack was old enough to drive, he and his buddies could venture a bit farther away, and Mammoth and Sun Valley were likely destinations. During his college days, skiing became more and more of a factor, and he decided to become a dentist so he could take a day off during the week to ski. Dental School never happened, and

Boomer Devaurs and Jack Pieroni—two legends of the China Peak-Sierra Summit ski world—share a smile on a great winter Sunday. *Photo courtesy Sierra Summit collection.*

like many skiers, his life took a different turn. Dentistry's loss is the ski industry's gain.

The offer of a job at Mid-Valley Sports in 1952 was too good to pass up, so Jack left college and started a long career in retail sports. He was with Mid-Valley Sports in downtown Fresno for 19 years. He left that to start his own business, Jack Pieroni Ski and Sports, in Fig Garden Village in 1971. He closed the doors in 1986, and went to work for his old friend, Herb Bauer, in 1986, and he is still there.

Jack is the expert to ask any ski questions, so with that thought in mind, we sat down and talked about what products had the most influence in improving skiing in the last fifty years. Jack scratched his head a bit, thought seriously, and found it hard to narrow to just three. Head Skis had to be on the top; and we agreed. Heads were the first to combine wood, plastic, and aluminum, and that led to all the competing ski companies playing catch-up to match them. Jack remembered one day when Howard Head drove up to Mid-Valley Sports in his Chrysler, with sample skies strapped to the roof.

The number two improvement had to be the transition from lace-up leather boots to buckle boots, and finally, plastic boots. Jack said he had calluses on his fingers from lacing up boots that customers were trying on. One boot company had the motto in 1960, "Are you lacin' while others are racin'?"

Gore-Tex filled the number three spot. It came on the scene in 1969, and from then on we could stay dry. Snow wiped off and did not soak through the clothing.

The list goes on and on, Jack says: safe bindings, ski-brakes, better grooming on the hills. All these contributed to make skiing safer and more pleasant. Jack still works in the industry, and skis every Sunday. He will forever, I guess.

CHAPTER 10

The Faithful Employees

BRIAN BRESSEL

Brian has been general manager of Sierra Summit since Pete Scaparo left the company in 2001. Brian had been Pete's right-hand man as his assistant manager. Pete described Brian as "the man I turned to when I needed it done," and that sums up Brian perfectly.

He has been in charge of the resort during the years of sustained growth, guiding the ship carefully, avoiding the financial icebergs, steering a cautious course between expansion and profitability. The general manager is responsible to the corporate headquarters for profits and loss. He is also responsible to the U.S. Forest Service; it is the landlord, and it writes the rules, because Sierra Summit is a Permit Holder on public land. The Permit Holder is answerable to the Forest Service, and it must treat public land respectfully. No changes can be made to the land without the specific permission of the Forest service.

Brian started as a National Ski Patroller at China Peak in 1978. He became a pro patroller three years later while still attending Fresno State. After graduating with a BS degree, he worked his way into management. He was in charge of purchasing when Pete moved him to the assistant manager position.

Brian is not the only Bressel to work at Sierra Summit, not by a long shot. Brian's mother, father, sister, and three brothers have worked there, too. His mother, Joanna, was hired in 1980, to establish the first day care center at China Peak.

Brian has been Sierra Summit general manager since 2001; he was formerly assistant manager. He is a long-time employee, starting as a ski patroller in 1978, and has worked his way to the top job. He is an excellent skier, and like all the management staff, he is dedicated to providing the visiting skier and snowboarder with the finest skiing conditions.

Her husband, Frank, volunteered to build six baby cribs. Athena, Brian's older sister, was a ski instructor; his brothers, Cary, Derrick, and Eadric, were all patrollers.

Frank started working in the rental shop, fitting skis and boots for customers, and then moved into the repair shop. He has been the manager of the repair shop for many years. His little shop is now a separate building between the Day Lodge and the ski school. He is the guy you take your skis to for tune-ups and service.

PAUL GRAY, DIRECTOR OF MAINTENANCE
JENNIFER GRAY, SKI SCHOOL DIRECTOR

The ski resort operates a colossal amount of machinery, all of which is exposed to the most extreme weather conditions imaginable, and all must be dependable. Seven chairlifts,

The Bressel family has had more family members who were Sierra Summit employees than any other family. Frank the dad, is a ski mechanic, Athena, their daughter, is a former ski instructor, and Joanna the mother, heads up the kiddy day care facility. Athena's brother, Brian is general manager, and three other brothers, Cary, Derrick, and Eadric, were all patrollers. The family is very active in sports; they are shown here at the annual Father's Day Run.

one T-bar, two handle tows, and one moving sidewalk, six or more snowcats, eight snowmobiles, one front loader, two snowplows, a D-6 dozer and several trucks and company cars. All of this equipment requires constant maintenance. The chairlifts require daily inspections even before they are loaded with passengers. Any breakdowns seriously compromise safety and must be avoided. Paul is responsible for a staff of technicians that ensure lift safety, and mechanics that keep all of the equipment operating. During the summer of 2008, a new vehicle maintenance shop was built, with a heated floor so the mechanics could work on the vehicles indoors for the first time since the resort was built more than fifty years ago. All maintenance had been done outdoors in the weather until then.

Paul's hometown is London, England, and his friendly voice has a slight cockney accent. That is not too unusual, because the Sierra Summit's winter staff is truly international, with employees coming from the far corners of the globe. His early life started as an insurance underwriter, training with Lloyd's of London. He moved to California in 1986, and took a job at Sierra Summit as a lift operator, with plans to stay one year. He went on to become a lift mechanic and from there, moved on up the proverbial ladder to supervisor, then, head of all the resort's maintenance. Paul is responsible for hiring and training the lift maintenance and operating crew, and the vehicle maintenance crew.

Ski School Director Jennifer Gray, like many of the other department heads, has worked her way to the top. She started as an instructor in 1987 and moved into the director position in 2002. The ski school has always had outstanding directors and she has had big boots to fill; she has done an excellent job. Her responsibilities include hiring ski and snowboard instructors from around the world. She is responsible for evaluating their skill levels, and seeing that they maintain safety on the hill. It is her responsibility to ensure that Sierra Summit students are getting the best possible training. All of her instructors teach to Professional Ski Instructors Association standards.

Sometime along the way, he met a beautiful young ski instructor named Jennifer Kelley, and the rest is history. They were married in 1988, and have two children.

Jennifer Gray is now Ski School Director. She started as an instructor in 1987, and has worked her way up to the top ski school position. When Ski School Director Colin Baldock went to Yosemite as their new director in 2002, Jennifer was selected to fill the vacant position. She hires, trains, and oversees the ski and snowboard instructors, ensuring that they are qualified to teach according to standards set forth by the National Ski Instructors Association, as well as Sierra Summit's own high standards. Her instructors must stress safety, as well as making sure the students enjoy their training. Good instructors are made, not born. They arrive with their certifications, but must be nurtured to be successful and popular with their students. Jennifer makes sure they are not only qualified to teach at Sierra Summit Ski School, but that they treat students with courtesy and respect. Skiers who learn the basics are safer skiers, and will return to Sierra Summit to enjoy the sport for many years.

BOOMER DEVAURS

For some people, the name "Boomer" receives instant recognition. He is seldom called by his proper name, Patrick. It is Boomer's voice that you hear on the snow report or on the recorded message at the office. He started as ski instructor at China Peak in 1973 and worked his way up to marketing director. He is responsible for advertising; special promotions and season pass sales. He created the Host Program, with volunteer hosts and hostess to answer guest's questions and give directions. Boomer, like all of the top management staff at Sierra Summit, is an expert skier. It may not be required for the job, but it sure helps.

Boomer Devaurs is the marketing director for Sierra Summit. A long-time employee, he started as a ski instructor in 1973. His voice is the one you hear on ski reports, and it is Boomer that does the news interviews with the TV folks. More comfortable on skis than in front of cameras, Boomer is fast and smooth. If you ever have a chance to ski behind Boomer, take it, and watch an expert make the most difficult runs look like pieces of cake. He is tops! *Photo courtesy Sierra Summit collection.*

CHUCK DODDS

When the conversation turns to faithful, longtime employees, just think Chuck! He started as a pro patroller in 1970, and has worked every ski season since. He has the record as the longest serving patroller, hands down. Chuck's summers were spent as a paramedic, but the ski season has always been his favorite.

BRUCE AND STEVE GILLETT

Sierra Summit operates a full service hotel, The Summit Inn, with a dining room and bar, as well as food service, and a bar at the Day Lodge and Mainline Station. Midway has sandwiches, beer, and wine. All of these hospitality areas are under the direction of Steve Gillett, better known as

Long time pro patroller Chuck Dodds takes a moment's rest beside Academy in this February 21, 2000 shot. Chuck began his long career as a pro patroller at China Peak in 1969, and has worked every season since. Not only is Chuck a fantastic skier, he is also a paramedic and is dedicated to helping the injured.

"Stevo," the older of the two Gillett brothers. He has been with China Peak/Sierra Summit since 1972 (except for a few years when he ran a pizza parlor in Shaver Lake). In addition to Stevo's duties as Food Service Director, he is also very artistically talented, and is responsible for many of the signs and artwork that decorates the resort.

Stevo was originally hired to work in the ski rental and repair shop, and when he needed help in the winter of 1972–1973, he called in his younger brother, Bruce. After a year or two, Stevo moved over to food service, and left Bruce to manage the six employees and two-hundred pairs of skis. Bruce has been a yearly employee ever since. The repair–rental department has undergone many changes in size and style

Bruce Gillett, an employee since 1972, is the Rental Shop Manager. He started when the shop had 200 sets of skis, boots and poles to rent; now it has 1200 ski-sets, and 800 snowboards. On busy weekend days, every ski and board is on the hill. Beside him is his wife Dawn; and the little dog is Kayla, a fixture in the shop.

since Bruce assumed the management. All of the remodeling and reorganization was done by Bruce and his staff. From the 200 sets of skis, boots, and poles in 1972, the shop now has 1200 ski sets and 800 snowboards for rental.

CHAPTER 11

Looking Forward and Backward

C rystal balls are cheap, and Fresno has no shortage of palm readers and fortune tellers. Perhaps we would do well to consult some of these experts to forecast the next season's snowfall. Will skiers and snowboarders still come to our mountain to enjoy its majesty in the years to come? Will the winter sports grow, or will they stagnate while the thrill-seekers turn to something new? Is there a point at which the cost that must be charged for a ticket becomes beyond the reach of the avid followers of our sport? Will Sierra Summit provide an adequate profit to its owners to continue as a viable enterprise? What improvements are needed to serve the ski public? What does it take to entice families to come from cities farther away?

Dick Kun, the president of Snow Summit Ski Corporation, the owner of Sierra Summit, discussed these very topics with me in the summer of 2008, and perhaps, just perhaps, I can offer some insight to my readers.

Throughout the twenty-eight years that it has owned the resort, the Snow Summit Ski Corporation has added improvements every year, and will continue to do so. A new maintenance shop is being built this summer, to move snow-cat and vehicle maintenance indoors and out of the weather for the first time in over fifty years. Bulldozer work continues to improve runs and trails to make them more ski-friendly when the snow coverage is thin. Painting, cleanup, redecorating, and general repairs are a continuing process.

Will the resort continue to grow and become a year-round playground? It probably will not. While Sierra Summit offers

R.V. spaces year-round, most campers prefer the solitude of the Huntington Lake campsites. The vacationer who is looking for entertainment, whether it is shopping, gambling, fine dining or golf must look over another hill, because these amenities do not exist here. The resort enjoys the loyal following of the people of Central California, and although out-of-state skiers are welcome to enjoy the local hospitality, the customer base continues to come from close to home. Most skiers are day visitors, and return home after a day of skiing.

The Sierra Summit Ski area will probably not expand much farther, although there is some room for expansion to the east included in the Special Use Permit. Skier traffic does not justify more lifts and runs at this time. More improvements will be made to the existing snowmaking system to make all runs more skiable. Snowboarding is here to stay; there will be more challenging terrain designed for them. It seems that we work to make runs smooth, and then create obstacles for snowboarders to test their skills and offer a space for their exhibitions. There will be more marketing to young people in the future. The school programs that the local schools participate in to teach kids to ski are extremely valuable, and will continue as a good way to introduce young people to winter sports. Many of these kids would not have the opportunity if it were not for these programs.

Sierra Summit will continue to attract most of its skiers from Fresno and the San Joaquin Valley, but Bakersfield, San Luis Obispo, and Santa Maria are well represented, too. There will be more marketing directed at those cities and the Bay Area in the future.

The Snow Summit Ski Corporation is satisfied with Sierra Summit, and has no intentions to sell it or change the management.

THE PAST

I have made an honest attempt to weave a bundle of facts into a bouquet of a story. Many of the tales I have related here were gleaned from newspaper articles, personal interviews, and my own fading memories. The characters in my story are real. Most have been personal friends whom I have known for years. We have skied Sierra Summit, and before that, China Peak, on sunny days and days of storms. We have shared the sun-deck, drank the wine, told lies about the speed of our runs, and the depth of the snow banks we crashed. The stories of our daring jumps grew most grand with each glass. During my days as a ski instructor, we talked of the beautiful girls in our class. How could I forget those days in the eighties when the Radio City Rockettes were performing a Christmas program in Fresno? The entire entourage came to Sierra Summit for ski lessons and my class was filled with Rockettes! Naturally, a good instructor should be ready to help a poor girl in distress, so I did my best. They all looked so good in ski pants and tight sweaters; what a shame they were better dancers than skiers.

I now yearn for the old days as any old man is wont to do, yet I have no regret … none. I have skied China Peak when there was but one lonely payphone. Now, everybody on the lift has a cell phone stuck to his ear. Cars used to have to be chained up at the first flake of snow. Now, my AWD Honda never even slows down on Tamarack Grade. Blue jeans that got sopping wet have long been replaced by Gore-Tex ski pants that keep me warm and dry. My long wooden Northland skis that took brute strength to turn have now been replaced by Pocket-Rockets that turn with the slightest hint. All the skier has to do is think about making a turn, and the skis turn. Wooden skis belong over fireplaces to remind us of days that are long gone. And good riddance!

How can one forget the camaraderie of my fellow ski instructors, the long evenings in the bar that often led to dangerous fun? Hitching a ride behind the snowcats to the top of the mountain and skiing down by moonlight, or how about trying to ski without skis, using cafeteria trays instead? Strange, but some way, somehow, we all survived.

Things are more businesslike now, and that is certainly for the better.

From an old China Peak/Sierra Summit ski bum, I wish you happy skiing on our magnificent mountain, and let me remind you to keep your weight on your downhill ski.

Credits

This little book could not have been possible without the help of my wife Denise, who has spent countless hours encouraging me to continue writing when I wanted to go skiing.

My thanks must be extended to my friend and editor, Linda Robertson, who knows how to turn my randomly written words into real sentences with subjects and verbs.

To Janice Stevens, whose "Wednesday Writers" group has opened the door to literary success for many of us first-time wanabe writers, I say thank you, with all my heart for your never-ending encouragement.

I extend my special thanks for the help from the Snow Summit Ski Corporation President, Richard Kun.

This book would never have been possible without the cooperation of the management and staff of Sierra Summit who submitted to my endless quest of the facts. Thank you for letting me interview these folks when they should have been working.

Brian Bressel

Rich Bailey

Patrick "Boomer" Devaurs

Bruce Gillett

Steve Gillett

Paul Gray

Jennifer Gray

Phil Kerridge

Michael Nolen

The many stories and pictures of China Peak from the early days until 1974 were furnished by Joe and Joanne Weirick. They have been helpful and kind. They welcomed me most graciously into their home and shared the family album with me.

My thanks to Gary Bagdasarian for his candid interview and explanation of the Harris-Bagdasarian years.

The story of Otto Tamm and the Estonian ski club was furnished by his daughters, Kati Tamm and Tiina Tamm Dudley. They gave me complete access to their family scrapbook and allowed me the use of beloved family photographs.

Jack Pieroni has been so very generous to allow time to tell me his tales of early day China Peak, and his lifetime in the retail ski business. His years of dedication to the sport and the people who enjoy it are invaluable to the history.

Fritz Mlekusch and Richard Hudson deserve my gratitude for sharing stories of the early days of China Peak Ski Patrol.